Hands-On
Writing Activities

That Get Kids Ready for the **Writing Assessments**

By Susan Van Zile

SCHOLASTIC
PROFESSIONAL BOOKS

New York • Toronto • London • Auckland • Sydney
Mexico City • New Delhi • Hong Kong • Buenos Aires

Acknowledgments

This book is dedicated to the joy of teaching and learning and to Divine Inspiration, which fills our lives with wonder and surprise.

To my creative, talented students, who give me great hope for the future.

To Grandma Jean for her unconditional love, support, and faith.

To my colleagues for their generosity, gifts, and talents.

To Virginia, Terry, Ernie, Dick, Adam, and Karen for being visionaries and nurturing, compassionate human beings.

To the Cumberland Valley School District for fostering professional growth and development.

To my parents for their belief in education.

To the three bests in my life: Phil, Caroline, and Taylor. I love you.

Scholastic Inc. grants teachers permission to photocopy the designated reproducible pages from this book for classroom use. No other part of this publication may be reproduced in whole or in part, or stored in a retrieval system, or transmitted in any form or by any means, electronic, mechanical, photocopying, recording, or otherwise, without written permission of the publisher.
For information regarding permission, write to Scholastic Inc., 555 Broadway, New York, NY 10012.

Cover design by Josué Castilleja
Interior design by Sydney Wright
Interior illustrations by Kate Flanagan
ISBN 0-439-17542-9

Copyright © 2001 by Susan Van Zile
All rights reserved.
Printed in the U.S.A.

Table of Contents

Introduction

What's Inside—and Why

My goal in creating the hands-on activities in this book was to find meaningful and engaging ways to introduce students to the writing process, paragraph structure, and the three modes of writing (narrative, informational, and persuasive). The activities were designed to incorporate the multiple intelligences, encourage active learning, develop thinking skills, consider current brain research, and address national and state standards. My hope is that your students will enjoy and learn as much from them as my students have.

The activities in Chapter One introduce students to the writing process and the multiple intelligences. Because writing is a process and because students need to reflect on their own writing processes, activities that introduce students to the steps in the process and encourage metacognitive reflection are

The Writing Process

Within the last two decades the paradigm for teaching writing has shifted from viewing writing as a "product" to perceiving it as a "process" (Calkins, 1986). Although the terminology they use to define the steps of the writing process differs somewhat, most researchers agree that writing is not a linear process; it is a recursive one. Regie Routman reflecting on her own writing process, captures its essence:

"I never go neatly through the steps; I meander back and forth through stages. I percolate, write a draft, revise, percolate, rewrite the draft, percolate, begin a new draft, revise a previous draft some more, and so on. I don't follow any sequential steps. I let the writing—and what I think I might want to say—lead me. As much as possible, we need to allow students the same time and latitude to find out what works for them" (Routman, 1991).

essential at the start of the school year. Students begin by creating writing autobiographies to examine their experience with writing. I invite them to use a multiple intelligences project (see page 14) to share their experience.

(see page 14)

In Chapter Two, students, now familiar with the writing process, utilize it to compose

> ## Multiple Intelligences
>
> Howard Gardner defines the eight intelligences as verbal-linguistic, math-logic, spatial, musical, bodily-kinesthetic, interpersonal, intrapersonal, and the naturalist. Simply stated, human beings have the capacity to be word smart, logic smart, picture smart, music smart, body smart, people smart, self smart, and nature smart (Armstrong, 1994).

paragraphs. They begin with a verbal and visual analogy—comparing the structure of a paragraph to a cookie—and culminate with a bodily-kinesthetic activity in which they use Legos to construct a model of a paragraph. Chapter Two also contains several mini-lessons created to teach students how to identify the parts of a paragraph and how to write a paragraph.

Some of the strategies and activities for teaching paragraph structure that are included here begin at the *knowledge level* of Bloom's taxonomy. For example, students are at the knowledge level when they use a cookie as their visual prompt and think about how this cookie is related to what they already know about the paragraph. Students ascend to the *comprehension level* as partners take turns explaining the relationship between the parts of the cookie and the parts of a paragraph. Students reach the *application level* when they apply their knowledge of paragraph structure to create paragraphs during the Great Paragraph Race. In the Paragraph Detective activities, the class orally compares and contrasts different kinds of paragraphs, and then draws a Venn diagram showing the similarities and differences. In this manner students operate at the *analytic level* of

Bloom's taxonomy and also discover the three types of paragraphs: narrative, informational, and persuasive.

In Chapter Three I demonstrate how I use food inventions to teach students about narrative, informational, and persuasive writing. Within this chapter, I also provide the directions for the invention activity, photographs of students' inventions, teacher and student writing models that

Bloom's Taxonomy

Knowledge: recall information

Comprehension: grasp the meaning of information

Application: use the information

Analysis: break down the information into its parts

Synthesis: put together the information in new or different way

Evaluation: make a judgment about the information

illustrate how to use the food inventions as writing prompts, and a rubric designed to evaluate all three types of writing.

Because I believe that students learn through collaboration, most of the activities are designed for cooperative groups of four. The criteria I use to form mixed, balanced groups are academic ability, gender, ethnicity, current social skills, and learning styles. Since the activities are collaborative in nature, I have included copies of direction sheets that designate specific roles for individuals within the group. The sheets are structured to provide for individual accountability. After I have explained the project and modeled how to do it, I distribute one copy of the direction sheet to each group. Students then refer to the sheet to complete the activity in the amount of time allotted. Where appropriate, I also include examples of student products and the rubrics I use to evaluate them.

The hands-on activities included in this book should be used as introductory mini-lessons to create a firm foundation upon which a dynamic writing program can be built. As students engage in the activities to learn about fundamental writing concepts, they are active learners and participants who build, create, think, and compose. Moreover, they have fun while they are learning and often can't wait for class to start! To me, the most important aspect of this hands-on approach to writing is the students' enthusiastic responses. One morning as a student stood outside my door waiting for me to dismiss my class, I heard her exclaim, "Wow! What are we doing today? It smells like peanut butter in there." As she energetically entered the room smiling broadly, I wanted to tap dance on the table. What a great way to begin class!

Brain Research and Learning

"The brain learns best when it 'does' rather than when it 'absorbs'" (Tomlinson and Kalbfleisch, 1998). When students use Legos to design a model of a paragraph, they are "doing" rather than "absorbing," and thereby increase their chances of retaining information. To attach further sense and meaning to what they have absorbed about the process of writing a paragraph and the steps involved, students, through a written response, summarize what they have learned. This reflection and metacognition encourages active processing (Caine and Caine, 1990) and facilitates retention of an important concept: paragraph structure and composition. As brain research suggests, teaching that is based on concepts as opposed to facts is absolutely essential (Tomlinson and Kalbfleisch, 1998).

Meeting Language Arts Standards

The activities in this book directly support both national and state standards. The National Standards for the English Language Arts specify that "students employ a wide range of strategies as they write and use different writing process elements appropriately to communicate with different audiences for a variety of purposes." Standard 1 states that students should demonstrate competence in the general skills and strategies of the writing process. Standard 2 states that students should demonstrate competence in the stylistic and rhetorical aspects of writing.

CHAPTER ONE

The Writing Process

The Writing Autobiography

Since recent brain research indicates that "a person's physical and emotional well-being are closely linked to the ability to think and to learn effectively," educators need to create an "atmosphere of trust and intellectual safety" (Southwest Educational Development Laboratory, 1997) in which students' ideas, opinions, and feelings are valued and respected. While I have always worked to create a positive classroom climate for my students, I continue to try to improve, particularly in the area of teaching writing.

I try to assess students' writing at the beginning of the year to identify what the students already know and what they need to learn. I use writing surveys or diagnostic prompts that ask them to write a letter to next year's incoming sixth graders describing the trials and tribulations of the first week of middle school.

As a result of my sabbatical research, I have made some changes. In an effort to establish an emotionally safe environment where students can feel free to take risks, I also ask them to create a writing autobiography. I have several objectives. First, I want to know what my students' attitude is toward writing. Second, I want to know about the kinds of writing they have done, the kind they enjoy, and what kind challenges them and why. Finally, I want students to know how I felt about writing when I was in sixth grade, and I want to demonstrate writing about this experience in front of them. By taking risks and sharing my experiences with students, I hope to establish an atmosphere of trust and show them that, yes, even English teachers need to learn how to write.

To begin this assignment, I ask students to think about their experiences with writing and use questions to stimulate thinking. "What kind of experiences have you had with writing? Do you consider yourself a writer? Why or why not?" Next, I have students do a five-minute free write in which they express their thoughts and feelings about writing. When they finish, I ask them to share some of their thoughts with the class.

After the discussion, I tell students that I spent time thinking about my sixth grade experiences as a writer, and that I would like to share part of my own writing autobiography with them. As I begin talking about my experiences, I start composing on the overhead transparency, thinking aloud so that my students hear me verbalizing my writing process and understand why I cross things out or move them around. When I reach an appropriate point in my story, I stop writing and explain to students that I would like them to share their writing autobiographies with me so that I can see where they are with their writing. I ask everyone to write honestly and freely about their writing experiences. I also assure them that sharing these pieces with the class is optional.

After providing sufficient time for my students to write, I share the rest of my writing autobiography with the class, which I have included here as a guide to— not as a model of—the kind of information I want to glean from their work.

Pain, Joy, and Plain Hard Work
My Sixth Grade Writing Autobiography

In sixth grade, I was a hooked, left-handed writer. I still am. When I wrote in ink or tried to do beautiful calligraphy in art class, the flat side of my left hand smeared ink everywhere. From the kindness of his heart, the art teacher gave me a D on my calligraphy project.

To help me with my "hooked" hand, the classroom teacher used to sit at my desk and hold it straight, which made writing a laborious process. When Mrs. S. sat next to me, my face burned; my palms sweated; even my legs were beet red. I had been writing with a hook for so long that no matter how many times Mrs. S. had me rewrite my papers, I couldn't get "unhooked." Because of this experience, I hated to write. For me writing was pure torture. My stomach did flips whenever I heard Mrs. S. say, "It's time for our weekly composition." I felt like I was going to throw up.

One Friday after hearing the infamous words, "It's time to write," and experiencing my usual initial discomfort, my ears perked up because I was interested in the assignment Mrs. S. was describing. "Close your eyes and picture the most beautiful place in the world. Your mind is a camera. Photograph the sights. Where are you? What colors do you see? What objects surround you? What do you hear? Smell? Taste? Touch? What makes this environment so special?"

While Mrs. S. was speaking, I could clearly see the emerald green hills of a mountain in Hawaii called the Sleeping Giant. I zoomed in on the surroundings with my mind's camera and felt as if I were back on the island of Maui again.

As soon as I started to write, the words flowed from my pen like paint on a canvas. I couldn't seem to write enough about the gorgeous image that appeared in front of me. Before I knew it, the bell had rung, and it was time for the next class. I had written four full pages, and I had loved every minute of it, smears and all!

At home that night, I reread what I had written. Wow! I felt proud of my work for the first time in my life. I wondered what Mrs. S. would think. I took extra care with my handwriting and made sure to straighten my hook.

The following Friday, I had butterflies in my stomach as I waited for Mrs. S. to return our compositions. This piece mattered to me; I had tried my best and wanted to do well. When it was time for English class, Mrs. S. remarked, "Many of you wrote excellent essays. I could picture the places you described very clearly in my mind, and I enjoyed reading these. I'd like to read one of these compositions to you now."

As soon as Mrs. S. began reading, I recognized my work. Although I could feel my face flush and turn crimson, I felt proud and excited. When I heard a few of my classmates mutter, "Whoa!" at the end of the piece, I knew I had finally written a good story.

When I thought about my experience as a sixth grade writer, I discovered that I could write well when I felt personally connected to the topic. Then I had something to say. When I could not relate to the topic, or when the emphasis was on neatness, writing became a painful process. I also discovered that writing about my sixth grade experience felt soothing, healing, almost like a balm. It freed me to begin anew and to see my students and writing differently. As Atwell (1986) states, "Writers are vulnerable. That's the writer there on the page, his or her essential self laid bare for the world to see." By sharing my own vulnerabilities with my students, I hope to create an environment that frees them, too, and encourages them to risk becoming writers.

Visualizing the Writing Process Through Guided Imagery

Recent brain research indicates that "learning always involves conscious and unconscious processes" (Southwest Educational Development Laboratory, 1997). To encourage "active processing" educators must help students "consciously review" their individual writing process through "reflection and metacognition" (Southwest Educational Development Laboratory, 1997). To do this, I begin with guided imagery. I set the stage by bringing in a laundry basket full of materials from home that show my writing process. I spread them out on a long table in front of my classroom. In my pile of goodies, I include examples of prewriting, drafting, revising, and editing. I also have a completed manuscript with me, the precursor to the published book.

Naturally, the students are curious about the items on the table. I encourage them to examine the materials and ask questions. "How can you read this scribble, Mrs. V.Z.?" a student asks. I respond, "To me, that scribble is how I draft. I've tried to draft on the computer, but the paper and pencil is such an integral part of my writing process, I can't break the habit."

After the students return to their seats, I ask them to close their eyes, use their mind's eye as a camera, and to visualize their writing process. Then, I slowly read the following to them:

Picture yourself as you begin writing. Where are you? Are you reclining in a comfortable pale-blue Lazy-Boy®, or sitting in a thickly cushioned swivel chair in front of your computer? Are you clutching a rich chocolate candy bar in one hand and your special think-and-write pencil in the other? Are you munching on buttery popcorn and sipping soda by the word processor? Maybe your angelic white

Persian or your soft, cuddly Yorkie is curled up in your lap as your favorite CD plays in the background.

How do you begin writing? Do you think, jot, pace the floor, go for a walk, lean on your elbow, tap your pencil, or search through the refrigerator before you begin? Do you draw, hum, or twist your hair? Or do you just start writing? Can you write in "the thick of it," as brothers and sisters slam doors, crank up the cartoons, or shout at each other? Or do you need silence and a quiet nook with tons of light streaming through the window?

As you write, do the words flow across the page or screen, or do you write, stop, think, and then write some more? Do you cross out, delete, scribble, or wad up and discard sheets of paper? Or do you just "get it down" and turn in whatever comes out? Once you have written something, do you review it and make changes? Do you read it aloud to yourself or ask someone else to give you feedback? Is this where the "hard work" begins, or do you just correct the spelling and punctuation? Do you ever throw away what you've written and start again? Do you share your writing, or do you prefer to keep it to yourself? For a few moments, think about your writing process. Visualize your environment and see yourself as you progress through each phase.

After I activate students' prior knowledge about their writing process through the guided imagery, I ask them to do a quick five-minute free write in which they describe their writing process as they visualized it. When students finish writing, I ask them to discuss, with a partner they choose, what their writing process is like. They may either read their free write to their partner, or they may verbalize their process. Through visualization and brainstorming, students are prepared for the multiple intelligences project.

Multiple Intelligences Projects

Because I believe it is important for students to reflect on their individual writing processes, I ask them to do a multiple intelligences project designed to facilitate metacognition. First, I have students complete a multiple intelligences question-naire, and I create activities to teach them about the multiple intelligences theo-ry. That way, before students embark on the writing process projects, they understand what the different intelligences are and what they mean. For these projects to be successful, this knowledge base is essential.

To introduce the assignment, I distribute a handout titled The Writing Process Projects (page 19) to every student. Each project on the list is keyed to one of the eight intelligences and requires students to demonstrate an understanding of the writing process. Next, I describe and show examples of student projects from the previous year. Sharing student models with the class makes the stan-dards for quality projects clear. After showing the models, I distribute The Writing Process Project Rubric (page 20) and review the criteria for evaluation: the quality of the product, ability to follow directions, content, and the presenta-tion and/or performance.

Name _____ Date _____ Section _____

The Writing Process Projects

All projects are due _____ and must include your name, date, section, and the title of the project. A completed rubric must accompany every project.

Choose one project only.

Verbal/Linguistic: Write a story, such as *A Day in the Life of a Pencil* , in which you narrate the writing process from the pencil's (or the writing object's) point of view. Describe your day as a student takes you through his or her writing process. Feel free to choose a different topic or point of view for your story, but be sure to check with the teacher for approval.

Math-Logic: Design a flow chart that demonstrates your writing process or create a recipe for your writing process. If you choose to write the recipe, include a list of ingredients and the directions for preparation.

Spatial: Using any artistic medium (pen and ink, collage, pop-ups, or photographs), visually represent the steps of your writing process.

Musical: Write and perform a rap that demonstrates your writing process. Raps may be taped or performed for the class. **Or** make a tape of various musical compositions that reflect your writing process. Include a paragraph with your tape that explains how the music relates to your writing process.

Bodily-Kinesthetic: Perform a dance that depicts your writing process. Clearly define the various stages in your writing process through movements and gestures. Dances will be presented to the class.

Interpersonal: With a partner, write a play or a skit that demonstrates your writing processes. One character in the skit should be the writer. The other character in the skit should be **the writing** or **the object doing the writing**. Show the relationship between the writer and the writing or between the writer and the writing implement as they engage in the writing process. All skits must be performed in front of the class.

Intrapersonal: Create a "Reflections Log" in which you compare your moods to the various parts of the writing process. If you choose, illustrate these reflections.

The Naturalist: Design a poster in which you compare your writing process to the growth of a plant or to a cycle in nature, such as the water cycle.

Name _____ Date _____ Section _____

The Writing Process Project Rubric

	Skilled			Needs Work	

This product is well-prepared. — Skilled 5 4 3 2 1 Needs Work

Teacher Student
_____ _____ On time.
_____ _____ Complete.
_____ _____ Prepared with care.

Student follows specific directions and instruction. 5 4 3 2 1
_____ _____ Follows directions carefully.

The product has appropriate content. 10 8 6 4 2
_____ _____ Demonstrates understanding of the steps involved in the writing process.

_____ _____ Effectively analyzes and describes the individual's writing process.

Presentation or performance of the project is appropriate and appealing. 5 4 3 2 1
_____ _____ Applies elements and principles of art, music, or speech.
_____ _____ Uses appropriate materials for construction or performance.

Teacher's Score _____ **Student's Score** _____

Student's Comments: _____

Teacher's Comments: _____

50-47 = Excellent   46-43 = Very good   42-40 = Fair   39-35 = Needs improvement   Below 35 = Redo

I let students work on the projects in class for three 40-minute periods and provide the following materials for them to use:

Construction paper	Scissors	Tape recorder
Poster-size oak tag	Markers and crayons	CD player
Composition paper	Glue sticks	
Rulers	Blank tapes	

Students have one week to complete their projects, so, if they do not finish them in class, they do them for homework. Then, they informally share their completed projects in groups of four. Students who have created skits, raps, or dances share them with the whole class. To allow students to critique their performances and to provide models of the performance for next year's class, I videotape them. I also use the school's digital camera to photograph the projects for students' portfolios. Through these projects, students show their talents and demonstrate an authentic understanding of their writing process. Here are some examples of projects.

This Writin' Thing
A Rap About My Writing Process

Hey, I gotta write
Somethin' today.
Inside I scream,
"Baby, no way!"

I sulk and storm around
For awhile.
I get an idea and
Start to smile.

I sit by the computer
All happy and glad.
This writin' thing
Ain't half bad.

I type five words
Then delete three.
This writin' thing,
Mercy me!
I type, read, revise;
It's quarter past four.
I've written half a page
But gotta have more.

I turn on some music,
Grab a little snack,
Head for the computer,
Tap, delete, tap.

By now I'm sweatin';
My brain is fried.
No wonder I'm hungry;
It's quarter past five!

I read the page
Change this and that.
It's time to print;
That's a fact!

The paper looks mighty fine,
Yeah, I'm proud
To call it mine.
But this writin' thing
Sure takes time.

Direct Instruction and Technology

We all need to employ common language and common symbols as we engage in the writing process, so once students have finished their writing autobiographies and have elaborated on their individual writing processes, I use direct instruction to reinforce the terminology and the basic concepts. I've successfully used a mnemonic device, created by my student teacher Jeremy Rega, to help students remember the five parts of the writing process (prewriting, drafting, revising, editing, and publishing).

Purple	**d**ragons	**r**oast	**e**vil	**p**enguins.
r	r	e	d	u
e	a	v	i	b
w	f	i	t	l
r	t	s		i
i		e		s
t				h
e				

While the parts of the writing process, such as revision, cannot be taught in a single lesson and must be addressed continuously throughout the year, I provide an overview of the process through a computer multimedia program called Astound® from Astound, Inc. In addition to enabling you to create text, images, sound effects, Quick Time movies, and interaction, Astound® has a time-line feature that lets you control when objects enter and leave the screen. When I use it to introduce my mnemonic, first the sentence appears, and then, separately, each part of the writing process enters the screen under the appropriate letter. Afterward a purple dragon dashes across the screen roaring at an evil-looking penguin that shrieks, "Ahhhh!"

Astound® is excellent for teaching the concept of revision. One of my slides illustrates the acronym **ARMS** and shows the symbols associated with this revision strategy:

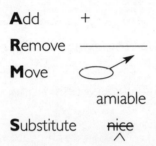

Add   +

Remove ——————

Move

                  amiable

Substitute   ~~nice~~

The next slide demonstrates how to apply ARMS to a sentence from a student's composition. First the sentence to be revised appears. Then, because of the time-line feature, one portion of the sentence is revised at a time. To make the revision, each of the editing symbols associated with ARMS is used. To provide students with immediate practice in revising, slides can be linked to one another: behind the slide illustrating revision I have a second slide with a sentence for students to revise. This technology tool has dramatically changed the way I teach the writing process and really grabs the students' attention. Teachers who do not have access to this kind of resource might create flash cards or transparencies that work on the same principle of illustrating the action, and then giving students a chance for practice. (See page 38 for a mini-lesson on ARMS.)

Throughout the year, I share audio and video tapes of famous authors talking about their writing and their writing processes. One video tape I highly recommend is titled *Writer's Solution: Writers at Work Video Tape* by Prentice Hall, which features writers like Jean Craighead George and Gary Soto. Another excellent source for connecting students to real authors who experience the same joys and frustrations they do is Scholastic's *Meet the Authors: 25 Creators of Upper Elementary and Middle School Books Talk About Their Work*. In addition, a web site that clarifies information about the writing process and describes various forms of writing can be accessed at: http://ccweb.norshore.webnet.edu/writingcorner/writingprocess.html.

The Writing Process Projects

All projects are due _____ and must include your name, date, section, and the title of the project. A completed rubric must accompany every project.

Choose one project only.

⬡ **Verbal/Linguistic:** Write a story, such as *A Day in the Life of a Pencil*, in which you narrate the writing process from the pencil's (or the writing object's) point of view. Describe your day as a student takes you through his or her writing process. Feel free to choose a different topic or point of view for your story, but be sure to check with the teacher for approval.

⬡ **Math-Logic:** Design a flow chart that demonstrates your writing process or create a recipe for your writing process. If you choose to write the recipe, include a list of ingredients and the directions for preparation.

⬡ **Spatial:** Using any artistic medium (pen and ink, collage, pop-ups, or photographs), visually represent the steps of your writing process.

⬡ **Musical:** Write and perform a rap that demonstrates your writing process. Raps may be taped or performed for the class. **Or** make a tape of various musical compositions that reflect your writing process. Include a paragraph with your tape that explains how the music relates to your writing process.

⬡ **Bodily-Kinesthetic:** Perform a dance that depicts your writing process. Clearly define the various stages in your writing process through movements and gestures. Dances will be presented to the class.

⬡ **Interpersonal:** With a partner, write a play or a skit that demonstrates your writing processes. One character in the skit should be the writer. The other character in the skit should be **the writing** or **the object doing the writing**. Show the relationship between the writer and the writing or between the writer and the writing implement as they engage in the writing process. All skits must be performed in front of the class.

⬡ **Intrapersonal:** Create a "Reflections Log" in which you compare your moods to the various parts of the writing process. If you choose, illustrate these reflections.

⬡ **The Naturalist:** Design a poster in which you compare your writing process to the growth of a plant or to a cycle in nature, such as the water cycle.

The Writing Process Project Rubric

This product is well-prepared.

Teacher	Student	
_____	_____	On time.
_____	_____	Complete.
_____	_____	Prepared with care.

	Skilled				Needs Work
	5	4	3	2	1

Student follows specific directions and instruction.

_____ _____ Follows directions carefully.

5	4	3	2	1

The product has appropriate content.

_____ _____ Demonstrates understanding of the steps involved in the writing process.

_____ _____ Effectively analyzes and describes the individual's writing process.

10	8	6	4	2

Presentation or performance of the project is appropriate and appealing.

_____ _____ Applies elements and principles of art, music, or speech.

_____ _____ Uses appropriate materials for construction or performance.

5	4	3	2	1

Teacher's Score   **Student's Score**

_____   _____

Student's Comments: _____

_____

Teacher's Comments: _____

_____

50-47 = Excellent   46-43 = Very good   42-40 = Fair   39-35 = Needs improvement   Below 35 = Redo

CHAPTER TWO

The Paragraph

Mini-Lesson 1: Cookies and Paragraph Structure

Once students are familiar with the writing process, I introduce them to paragraph structure, the basic framework for writing. To begin teaching the parts of the paragraph, I show students a sandwich cookie and ask them how it is related to what they already know about a paragraph. This visual prompting is a "powerful aid to hemispheric integration and retention" (Sousa, 1995). Below is the lesson I use with my students.

Objectives: To introduce students to the parts of a paragraph by using analogy. To identify the parts of a paragraph.

Time: One 40-minute class period.

Materials:
- ❂ Sandwich cookies—one for each student
- ❂ Overhead transparency of the Sandwich Cookie Paragraph (page 43)
- ❂ Copies of Paragraphs and Sandwich Cookies (page 44) for each student
- ❂ Yellow, pink, and blue highlighters—one set per student
- ❂ Chart paper
- ❂ Markers

Step-by-Step

1. Show your students a sandwich cookie. Capture their attention by asking if they are hungry. You might even walk around the room with a fresh bag of

cookies and describe the cookies' rich, chocolaty flavor and thick, creamy filling. Ask them to close their eyes and picture similarities between the cookie and a paragraph. Have students list some of the similarities on a piece of paper and discuss their lists with a partner. Randomly call on students to share their comparisons and write the responses on a sheet of chart paper. Then draw conclusions about the similarities students find.

2. The sandwich cookie paragraph is an analogy that compares the parts of the cookie to the parts of the paragraph. Using the overhead projector, show the class the paragraph, Sandwich Cookie Paragraph, and then, distribute copies of Paragraphs and Sandwich Cookies to students. After you read the paragraph aloud, ask questions that help students identify the various parts of the paragraph. Have them locate, highlight, and label the topic sentence in yellow, the supportive details in pink, and the clincher sentence in blue. Then ask students to circle and label the transition words.

3. After discussing and highlighting each part of the paragraph, have students work in pairs to list five facts about it. Next, ask each pair to share its list with another set of partners, so they can add new facts to their lists.

Name _____ Date _____ Section _____

Sandwich Cookie Paragraph

Crunchy, creamy sandwich cookies and paragraphs share common ingredients. Like the top part of the sandwich cookie, a paragraph's topic sentence provides a delicious introduction to the main idea of the paragraph. Inside the paragraph, the rich, smooth filling, or the supportive details, support and develop the topic sentence. At the bottom of the cookie and at the end of the paragraph, the delectable experience ends with a final chocolaty crunch, or with a clincher sentence that restates the main idea in a powerful, new way. In summary, when biting into a scrumptious sandwich cookie, remember it has three parts just like a paragraph.

Name _____ Date _____ Section _____

Paragraphs and Sandwich Cookies

Read the paragraph below. Highlight and label its various parts. Circle the transition words.

Crunchy, creamy sandwich cookies and paragraphs share common ingredients. Like the top part of the sandwich cookie, a paragraph's topic sentence provides a delicious introduction to the main idea of the paragraph. Inside the paragraph, the rich, smooth filling, or the supportive details, support and develop the topic sentence. At the bottom of the cookie and at the end of the paragraph, the delectable experience ends with a final chocolaty crunch, or with a clincher sentence that restates the main idea in a powerful, new way. In summary, when biting into a scrumptious sandwich cookie, remember it has three parts— just like a paragraph.

With a partner, discuss what you know about the paragraph. List five or more facts about paragraphs on the lines below. Share your facts with another set of partners. Add any new facts you learn from them to your list.

_____
_____
_____
_____
_____
_____
_____
_____
_____

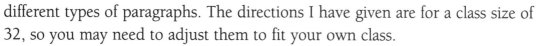

4. As a retention activity, invite partners to take turns explaining the relationship between the parts of the sandwich cookie and the parts of the paragraph. Provide a cookie as the reward for a correct explanation.

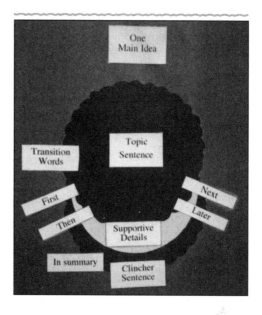

Mini-Lesson 2: The Great Paragraph Race

This is a game I use to reinforce the concept of paragraph structure and help students recognize characteristics of different types of paragraphs. The directions I have given are for a class size of 32, so you may need to adjust them to fit your own class.

Objectives: To determine the main idea of paragraphs.
To construct and analyze paragraphs.

Time: One 40-minute class period.

Materials Needed for Eight Groups of Four in a Class of 32:

> ✿ 8 laminated sets of different types of paragraphs:
>   2 narrative, 3 persuasive, and 3 informational
> ✿ 8 laminated sheets of blank paper
> ✿ 1 overhead projector marker for each group of 4
> ✿ 1 spray bottle filled with water for each group of 4
> ✿ Paper towels (3 or 4 per group)
> ✿ Masking tape or transparent tape (1 roll per group)
> ✿ Chart paper
> ✿ Construction paper
> ✿ Markers
> ✿ 9 folders
> ✿ Paper clips

Preparing the Activity

1. Choose two narrative, three persuasive, and three informational paragraphs. I use both paragraphs I have written and those written by former students. I have included three examples below.

2. On the computer, type one sentence of each paragraph per page, using 36- or 48-point type.

3. Print out the paragraphs. Make seven photocopies of each page and then laminate all the sheets. Laminate eight sheets of blank paper, too.

4. Collate the paragraphs into eight sets and secure them with a paper clip. Be sure the sentences are not in the correct order. Place the sets of paragraphs and blank laminated sheets in separate folders, numbered from 1 to 8. On the front of each folder, write the topic of the paragraph. Put the blank laminated pages in another folder and label "Main Idea Sheets."

5. Designate eight sections of the room as areas where students will hang their paragraph. I divide my blackboard into four sections, and use the back wall for the other four sections.

Three Examples of Paragraphs to Use

Example 1—A Narrative Paragraph

I was working on my English report at my desk in my bedroom one night when I heard a strange noise like a "grrr-hiss" coming from my closet. I was frightened and dashed downstairs to get my dad. When we came back to my room, the report I had left on my desk was gone, but a "grrr-hiss" was still coming from my closet. My dad yanked open the door, and there was a tiny, multicolored dragon sitting on my sneaker. The little fellow could not have been more than a foot tall. He had red eyes; silvery wings; a wriggly tail; and soft, silky fur colored ruby red, emerald, indigo, and violet

—Angela Benion, Grade 6

Example 2—A Persuasive Paragraph

The school board should not support year-round school. If we have year-round school, I will not be able to spend summers with my dad, who lives in California. A second reason I am opposed to year-round school is that I earn over two thousand dollars each summer because I mow lawns. If I cannot work in the summer, it will be difficult, if not impossible, for me to afford college. A third reason I am against year-round school is that I will not be able to participate in summer educational programs, such as Theater in the Park, because the rehearsals occur during the day. Because year-round school separates divorced parents from children, prevents students from earning income, and discourages students from participating in enrichment programs, I am against it.

Example 3—An Informational Paragraph

To make a scrumptious peanut butter ice cream pie, follow these steps. First, mix one and a half cups of crushed graham crackers, one-fourth cup of sugar, and half a cup of melted margarine together in a mixing bowl. Next, stir these ingredients and press them into a pie pan. Finally, blend together one quart of vanilla ice cream, one-half cup of chunky peanut butter, and half a cup of whipping cream. When the ice cream mixture is smooth, spoon it into the crust and freeze it for five hours before you enjoy it.

Step-by-Step

1. Divide the class into eight groups of four. Ask the students to arrange their desks in squares and assign themselves numbers from 1 to 4. These will be their "runner" numbers.

2. You can get your students motivated by announcing that they are about to participate in The Great Paragraph Race, in which will their intellectual skill and athletic prowess must be up to Olympic standards. A banner that says, "The Great Paragraph Race," hanging in the front of the classroom can help

set the mood, and you could even wear a referee's hat and a whistle.

3. Explain to students that each group will receive a set of laminated pages. Most of the pages will have sentences on them, and one will be blank. Each time they receive a set, they will do the following:

   A. Arrange the sentences in order so that they form a paragraph.

   B. Determine the main idea of the paragraph.

   C. Use the overhead projector marker to write the main idea on the blank laminated sheet.

   D. Send one runner at a time from the groups (for example, all the number 1's) to hang up the sentences and the paragraph's main idea in their designated area.

   E. The first group that has the sentences arranged in order and has the correct main idea gets two points. Each group with the correct response thereafter receives one point.

   F. After one round, one group member removes the main idea and paragraph from the hanging area. You can rotate this role by number. The group then discards the masking tape, scrambles the order of the sentences, clips them together, and returns them to the proper folder. Each group keeps the blank laminated sheet, but they need to clean it after each round, using the paper towels and spray bottles.

   Be sure to announce that each runner is also responsible for putting masking tape on his or her sentence so the sentences can be attached in order. The whole group assists with clean-up.

4. To prepare for the game, distribute to each group one spray bottle, one overhead projector marker, paper towels, masking tape, one blank laminated sheet, and one set of similar sentences. Place the sentences face down on the desks.

5. Before the game begins, explain to students that groups are disqualified from the race if:

   A. They are too noisy.

B. They flip their sentence cards face up before the teacher blows the whistle or calls out, "1, 2, 3, flip!"

C. They engage in unsportsmanlike conduct.

D. They send a runner before the previous runner is seated.

E. Their sentences fall down.

You may want to draw particular attention to this last point, since it means that care, as well as speed, is necessary.

6. Start the game by blowing the whistle or saying, "1, 2, 3, flip!" Repeat this signal each time you distribute a new set of cards.

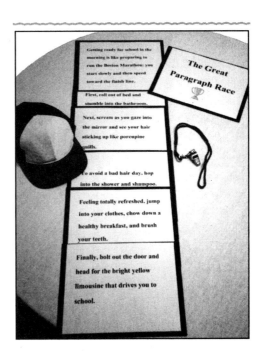

7. After each paragraph is hung, examine the main ideas. Compare and contrast them. Invite the students to explain how they determined the order of the sentences. Use an overhead projector marker to circle the transition words. Have students create a list of these transition words in their notebooks. Throughout the activity, reinforce the concepts of topic sentence, supportive details, and clincher sentence.

TEACHER TIP

Although the initial preparation for this activity is time-consuming, the results are worth the effort. Students love the active nature of this game, and they learn a tremendous amount about paragraph structure and the three kinds of paragraphs as we discuss them. Because I have found that student-generated paragraphs seem to work best for this activity, I photocopy—with student permission—examples of different types of student paragraphs throughout the year to use for the next year's race. It is fun for students to know that their learning materials were written by other students and that their work, too, might be used in a future lesson.

Mini-Lesson 3: Paragraph Detectives

Objective: To compare and contrast the different types of paragraphs.

Time: One 40-minute class period.

Materials:
- ○ Sandwich cookies—one for each student
- ○ 1 set of each of the laminated paragraphs used in The Great Paragraph Race
- ○ Masking tape
- ○ Chart paper
- ○ Markers
- ○ 1 copy of the Venn diagram (page 45) for each student
- ○ Overhead transparency of a Venn diagram

Step-by-Step

1. Before you start the lesson, hang the eight paragraphs (two narrative, three informational, and three persuasive) used in the relay race around the room. Next to each, place a piece of chart paper and a colored marker.

2. Tell the students that there are three different types of paragraphs in the room: narrative, informational, and persuasive. Ask them to define each type, based on what they already know about paragraphs.

3. Send the class on a "gallery tour" of the paragraphs. Begin by having students work in groups of four and assigning each group one of the paragraphs to read silently. After each group member has had a chance to read the paragraph, the group decides together whether it is narrative, informational, or persuasive, providing reasons for the choice. To continue the tour, say, "1, 2, 3, Move," and have the groups rotate clockwise around the room. Repeat this process until all groups have reread all eight paragraphs.

4. After the tour, point to each paragraph and ask students to state whether it is narrative, informational, or persuasive. Be sure they provide reasons for their choice. Based on the discussion, label the chart paper next to each paragraph narrative, informational, or persuasive.

5. Send the groups on a second gallery tour of the paragraphs. This time, tell them they are detectives on a hunt for the characteristics of the three types of paragraphs. Use the Sandwich Cookie Paragraph (page 43) to demonstrate what you want the students to do. Show the model on the overhead and ask students what kind of paragraph it is. Through questioning, guide them to understand that its purpose is to *inform* the reader about similarities between the cookie and the paragraph. Then, help students discover a few of the characteristics of informational writing, such as that it explains and informs and that it develops the main idea with specific examples and details.

6. As the students embark on this second gallery tour, they should review together the characteristics of each type of paragraph. Following the discussion, they can take turns writing one or two of their observations on the chart paper posted next to each paragraph, without repeating what previous groups have written.

7. After the tour, use the chart paper to help students generate a list of characteristics for each type of writing. Begin by sharing students' observations about similar types of paragraphs. As you list the characteristics of each type of writing on the board, have students write them on a sheet of paper to keep in their notebooks.

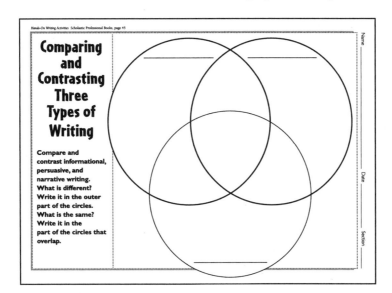

Hands-On Writing Activities Scholastic Professional Books, page 45

Comparing and Contrasting Three Types of Writing

Compare and contrast informational, persuasive, and narrative writing. What is different? Write it in the outer part of the circles. What is the same? Write it in the part of the circles that overlap.

Name:

Date:

Section:

8. Once your students have a firm grasp of the characteristics of the three modes of writing, distribute the Venn diagrams (page 45). Ask the students to use their notes and what they have read to compare and contrast the three modes of writing. They may either work with a partner, or complete the activity independently as homework.

9. As a class, discuss the Venn diagrams. Using the overhead transparency of the diagram, record students' observations.

TEACHER TIP

Another way to have students discover the characteristics of informational, persuasive, and narrative writing is through a jigsaw activity. Form three panels of experts, one for each mode of writing. Give each group two or more models of the type of writing they are to analyze. The groups should generate a list of characteristics of this type of writing and then use reference sources, such as grammar or composition books or appropriate Web sites, to refine their lists. Then, form jigsaw groups of three students. Include one student from the various expert groups. Use the experts to teach the other students about one of the three types of writing.

Mini-Lesson 4: Building Paragraph Models with Legos

To reinforce further what they have learned about paragraphs, students use Legos to build a model of a paragraph.

Objective: To demonstrate an understanding of paragraph structure by using Legos to construct a model of a paragraph and explaining the model to the rest of the class.

Time: One 40-minute period.

Materials Needed for Eight Groups of Four in a Class of 32:

- 8 bags of Legos, one per group; number each bag from 1 to 8
- 8 envelopes, one per group
- 8 index cards, one per group
- 8 pairs of scissors, one per group
- 8 rolls of transparent tape, one per group
- 8 pocket folders, one per group

Step-by-Step

1. Have students take two or three minutes to discuss, with a partner, everything they can remember about a paragraph.

2. Explain to students that they will be using Legos to build a model of something to represent the paragraph. Show them that they can use shapes and colors to represent the parts and ingredients of a paragraph. Instruct students to cut apart the index card to make labels that indicate which part of the paragraph each segment of their model represents. Provide an example of what you expect. I use the sandwich cookie paragraph as my model.

3. Form groups of four and ask students to number themselves from 1 to 4. Assign the following group roles:

   #1—Labeler. This person will:
   - Cut the index card apart to make as many labels as the group needs for its model.
   - Create labels for the various parts of the paragraph on the pieces of the index card.

▲ Tape the labels to the model.

#2—Reporter. The reporter will:

▲ Show the completed model to the class.

▲ Explain how the model relates to the paragraph.

#3—Gopher. The gopher will:

▲ Gather and return the materials.

▲ Write the Lego bag number and group members' names on the envelope.

▲ Remove the labels from the model after it has been shown to the class and place them in the envelope.

▲ Write the names of the group members on the front of the pocket folder.

#4—Sketcher. The sketcher will:

▲ Draw a picture of the model and label its parts.

All members of the group will participate in building the model.

4. Write the group directions on the board:

   A. As a group, decide what to build as your model. (3–5 minutes)

   B. Build the model. Each group member should build one section of it. (10–15 minutes)

C. Label the parts of the model. (3–5 minutes)

D. Draw a sketch of the model. Include the labels.

5. After the models are built, the reporters will share the models with the class and explain how each model relates to its paragraph.

6. Clean up the materials. You can store the envelopes containing the labels and the sketches of the models in the pocket folders.

TEACHER TIP

The first time you use this activity, students may need more than one class period to complete it. If they do not finish the activity in the designated amount of time and classes are changing, you will need to reserve a few minutes before the end of the period to clean up the materials. The next day have the gophers retrieve the same bag of Legos their groups used to build the original model. The group can then use their sketch of the model to rebuild it quickly. Since the labels are stored in the envelope, they can be taped to the model quickly, too.

Mini-Lesson 5: Super-Size Paragraphs

In this lesson, your students will work in groups to learn the relationship between paragraph structure and the models they built in Mini-Lesson 4 by reversing the process and writing a paragraph about the model.

Objective: To compose a paragraph showing the relationship between the paragraph and the Lego model students will work in cooperative learning groups.

Time: One to two 40-minute class periods.

Materials Needed for Eight Cooperative Groups in a Class of 32

- ⚙ 8 large paper clips
- ⚙ 8 rolls of masking tape, one per group
- ⚙ 8 off-white sentence strips
- ⚙ 24–34 sentence strips in a single color
- ⚙ 8 sentence strips in a second color
- ⚙ 32 markers
- ⚙ 8 pocket folders (use the same ones created in Mini-Lesson 4)
- ⚙ 8 Instruction Sheets for the Group Lego Project (page 46–47), one per group
- ⚙ 8 Prewriting Sheets for the Group Paragraph About the Lego Model (page 48)
- ⚙ 8 Rubrics for A Paragraph Is Like a ___ (page 49–50)
- ⚙ An overhead transparency of the rubric

Step-by-Step

1. Before class, place the three reproducibles inside the pocket folders.

2. Ask the students to form groups of four and assign themselves letters from A to D. Assign the following group roles:

Person A—The Task Master:
Writes the topic sentence.
Keeps the group on task.
Checks off the items on the Group Instruction Sheet as they are completed.

Person C—The Encourager:
Writes the second supportive detail.
Acts as the group's cheerleader.
Tells the group when it is doing well.
Motivates the group to do its best and to keep trying.

Person B—The Gopher:
Writes the first supportive detail.
Gathers and returns materials.

Person D—The Contributor:
Writes the third supportive detail.
Contributes ideas to the group.

Name _____ Date _____ Section _____

Instruction Sheet for the Group Lego Project

Objective: To write a group paragraph explaining the relationship between your Lego model and a paragraph.

Social Skill: Working together.

Group Members' Roles	Name of Group Member
Person A: Topic Sentence/Task Master	_____
Person B: Supportive Detail #1/Gopher	_____
Person C: Supportive Detail #2/Encourager	_____
Person D: Supportive Detail #3/Recorder	_____
Whole Group: Clincher Sentence	

Directions: Complete each of the steps below. Put a check mark in front of each item after you have completed it.

_____ 1. Assign the group roles. Fill in the name responsible for the role assigned.

_____ 2. Complete the sheet titled "Prewriting About the Lego Model." Take turns. B his or her job.

_____ 3. Send the gopher to get the following
  4 large markers
  1 off-white sentence strip
  3 pink sentence strips
  1 blue sentence strip
  1 large paper clip
  1 roll of masking tape

_____ 4. Using the marker, each group member sentence on the following sentence st
  Letter A—Topic Sentence (off-white s
  Write your name on the back.

Name _____ Date _____ Section _____

Prewriting Sheet for the Group Paragraph About the Lego Model

Directions: Each member of your group has been assigned a particular role. Complete this sheet by taking turns and writing your assigned sentence.

Topic Sentence: States the main idea of the paragraph; shows what your model and the paragraph have in common.

Letter A—Write the topic sentence here: _____
_____

Supportive Detail #1: Shows one way in which your model is like a paragraph. (Remember to use a **transition** word if you need it. Circle the transition word.)

Letter B—Write supportive detail #1 here: _____

second way that your model is similar to a
n supportive detail #1. (Remember to use a
hen circle it.)

ail #2 here: _____

third thing that your model and a paragraph have
om supportive details #1 and #2. (Remember to
d to, then circle it.)

ail #3 here: _____

s the main idea of the paragraph in a powerful,
ircle a **transition** word that signals the end of

her sentence here: _____

Name _____ Date _____ Section _____

Rubric for "A Paragraph Is Like a _____"

Group Members' Names: _____
Peer Editors' Names: _____

Write the score for each item in the appropriate blank. Total the scores at the end.

1. The model effectively demonstrates its relationship to the paragraph.

4	3	2	1
The model effectively demonstrates its relationship.	The model demonstrates some similarities.	The model demonstrates few similarities.	The model demonstrates no similarities.

Score: _____ Group _____ Peers

2. The model is labeled, neat, and detailed.

4	3	2	1
The model is labeled and is exceptionally neat and detailed.	The model is labeled and is neat and detailed.	The model is labeled but could be neater and more detailed.	The model looks as if it were thrown together at the last minute.

Score: _____ Group _____ Peers

3. The paragraph has a topic sentence that states the main idea.

4	3	2	1
The topic sentence is interesting and clearly states the main idea.	The topic sentence states the main idea.	The topic sentence does not clearly state the main idea.	There is no topic sentence or the topic sentence does not state the main idea.

Score: _____ Group _____ Peers

4. The paragraph has at least three supportive details that make clear comparisons between the parts of the model and the parts of the paragraph.

4	3	2	1
The three supportive details make outstanding comparisons.	The three supportive details make clear comparisons.	The three supportive details make unclear comparisons.	There are fewer than three supportive details, and/or they are unclear.

Score: _____ Group _____ Peers

The **Whole Group** writes the clincher sentence after rereading the paragraph.

3. Distribute the folders.

4. Explain to your students that they will compose a paragraph similar to the one about the sandwich cookie. In their paragraph they must show the similarities between their Lego model and the paragraph. The paragraph will be written by the group and shared with the class.

5. Ask students to remove the rubric titled A Paragraph Is Like a __ from the pocket folder. Review it with them on the overhead transparency to familiarize them with the criteria for evaluation. (Note: When students complete the final draft, they will draw a colored, labeled picture of their Lego model to answer the criteria for items one and two on the rubric.)

6. Ask students to remove the prewriting and group instruction sheets from the folder. With the Task Master's guidance, the students should then pass the prewriting sheet around the group in alphabetical order to complete it. As one student writes, the others, especially the Contributor, can offer suggestions for the various sentences.

7. After students review the prewriting sheet, they can begin composing their rough draft of the paragraph on the color-coded sentence strips. The topic sentence is written on the off-white sentence strip, the supportive details are written on one color strip, and the clincher is written on the second color strip. Send the Gopher to retrieve the materials listed on the group instruction sheet.

8. Number the groups from 1 to 8. Post numbered index cards or pieces of construction paper in eight sections of the room to indicate where each group should hang its completed sentence-strip paragraph. After students complete the rough draft of the paragraphs, they can tape their strips in the designated areas.

9. Students then go on a silent gallery tour of the paragraphs. To make sure the tour is effective, organize it with group #1 reading group #2's paragraph and group #8 reading group #1's. At your "1, 2, 3, move" signal, the groups rotate in numerical order.

10. What do students think about the writing? Ask them to identify the paragraphs they thought were well written and explain why. If a paragraph was not as effective as it could be, what improvements could be made? Why?

11. Clean up the materials. Clip sentence strips together. Store the sentence strips, instruction sheets, prewriting sheets, and the rubrics in the pocket folders.

TEACHER TIP

For this lesson to be effective, the teacher must confer with each group during the writing process. Because this activity involves higher-order thinking, the students may have some difficulty making detailed comparisons. For example, many write, "The roof of the house is a topic sentence." They do not explain how they are similar to one another. For younger students, or for those students with learning disabilities, you may want to change or adapt the writing assignment. The assignment needs to be related to the Lego model. The Prewriting Sheet for the Paragraph Model, version 2 (pages 51–52) is an adaptation of the assignment I use with learning disabled students and struggling writers to help them experience success and develop a positive attitude toward writing.

Name _____ Date _____ Section _____

Prewriting for the Paragraph Model Version 2

Directions: Each member of your group has been assigned a particular role. You must complete this sheet by taking turns and writing your assigned sentence.

Topic Sentence: States the main idea of the paragraph; shows what your model and the paragraph have in common.
Letter A. Create a topic sentence by filling in the blanks below.

A _____ has a lot in common with a paragraph.
 (what your model is)

Supportive Detail #1 Shows one way that your model is like a paragraph.
Letter B. Create supportive detail #1 by filling in the blanks below.

_____ the _____ is like
 (transition word)   (part of the model that is like the topic sentence of a paragraph)

the topic sentence of a paragraph because _____
_____
_____
_____
_____

Supportive Detail #2 Shows a second way that your model is similar to a paragraph. It must be different from supportive detail #1.
Letter C. Create supportive detail #2 by filling in the blanks below.

_____ the _____
 (transition word)   (part of the model that is like the supportive details)

represents the supportive details because _____
_____
_____
_____
_____

Mini-Lesson 6:
Using ARMS: A Revision Strategy

Revision is an important concept, and this lesson is an effective way to begin the process of teaching it. I start by explaining to my students that writing is not usually finished on the first try. To be its best, writing needs revision to emphasize the strengths and correct the weaknesses. The ARMS mnemonic will help them remember the strategy for revision.

The lesson takes two 40-minute periods to complete, so I have divided it into two parts.

Objective: To introduce the concept of revision and the revision strategy known as ARMS.

Time: Two 40-minute periods.

Materials: ✿ Overhead transparency of a paragraph to edit
✿ Pocket folders containing group instruction sheets, sentence strips, and sketches of the Lego model and the rubrics
✿ One copy of A Group Revision Activity (page 53) for each student

Step-by-Step for Period 1 of ARMS

1. Explain that writing is a process that takes time and effort both to teach and to learn. A revision strategy called ARMS is a way to begin the revision process. Use the bodily-

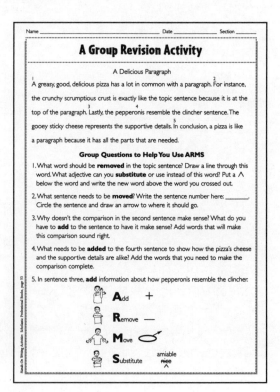

Name _____ Date _____ Section _____

A Group Revision Activity

A Delicious Paragraph

1 A greasy, good, delicious pizza has a lot in common with a paragraph. For instance, 2 the crunchy scrumptious crust is exactly like the topic sentence because it is at the 3 top of the paragraph. Lastly, the pepperonis resemble the clincher sentence. The 4 gooey sticky cheese represents the supportive details. In conclusion, a pizza is like 5 a paragraph because it has all the parts that are needed.

Group Questions to Help You Use ARMS

1. What word should be **removed** in the topic sentence? Draw a line through this word. What adjective can you **substitute** or use instead of this word? Put a ∧ below the word and write the new word above the word you crossed out.

2. What sentence needs to be **moved**? Write the sentence number here: _____. Circle the sentence and draw an arrow to where it should go.

3. Why doesn't the comparison in the second sentence make sense? What do you have to **add** to the sentence to have it make sense? Add words that will make this comparison sound right.

4. What needs to be **added** to the fourth sentence to show how the pizza's cheese and the supportive details are alike? Add the words that you need to make the comparison complete.

5. In sentence three, **add** information about how pepperonis resemble the clincher.

Add +

Remove —

Move ⟳

Substitute amiable / nice ∧

Hands-On Writing Activities Scholastic Professional Books, page 53

TEACHER TIP

Read through the drafts of the student Lego model paragraphs that are in the pocket folders and note any common errors the students may be making. To create a group revision activity, select a paragraph that contains these common errors. Ask the students' permission to use the paragraph for revision. Or you can create a paragraph that contains the errors. I have discovered that students need continuous practice with revision throughout the year. If you begin the process of revision as a group activity, it assists those students who either have little experience with revision or who have great difficulty revising their writing.

kinesthetic method to teach the ARMS acronym (see Chapter 1). Act like an Army drill sergeant as you loudly call out, "ARMS!" Tell students to stand at their desks, flex their muscles, and shout, "ARMS!" Then, have them respond with the following phrases and gestures.

	Phrase	Gestures
	Add	Make a "plus" sign with your arms
	Remove	Move your right arm horizontally in front of you, like a line striking through a word
	Move	Make circles with both hands going in opposite directions
	Substitute ~~nice~~ ^{amiable}	With both arms bent in front of you, move your left arm over your right.

You can repeat the phrases and gestures several times until students know them well enough to do them independently.

2. By thinking aloud, demonstrate on the paragraph transparency how to revise a paragraph with ARMS. (Providing students with copies of the paragraph allows them to revise it along with you.)

3. Form squares (groups of four) and distribute the sheet titled A Group Revision Activity to each student. Explain that this sheet is designed to guide them

through the revision process. Each member of the group answers one of the questions at the bottom of the sheet and revises the paragraph accordingly. All members of the group make the suggested revisions on their own sheets.

4. Show the paragraph students have been editing on the overhead and ask them to suggest changes.

Step-by-Step for Period 2 of ARMS

1. Distribute the pocket folders containing the group instruction sheets, sketches of the Lego models, and sentence strips.

2. Ask students to rehang their paragraphs in the designated places. Once the paragraphs are up, students should silently reread the paragraph. Then, they should revise it with ARMS, using a marker different from the original color.

3. When the revisions are completed, two group members should write the final copy on notebook paper or on the computer while the other two draw a detailed, color illustration of the group's paragraph model.

4. After the final copies are written, have the task master take the rubric for A Paragraph Is Like a __ from the pocket folder for group members to use in evaluating their paragraph. Pair two cooperative learning groups. Have them exchange paragraphs and rubrics, and evaluate each other's paragraphs. Below is an example of one group's draft and final product.

A Paragraph and an Ice Cream Cone
Draft Before Revising and Editing

The moist, creamy ice cream cone is a lot like a paragraph. The rich whip cream toping is the topic sentence. Because the topic sentence is rich with information about the paragraph. The cool texture of the ice cream is the supportive detail the supportive details are in the middle just like the ice cream. The crunchy cone is alot like the Clincher Sentence because the Clincher Sentence ends the paragraph just as the cone ends the Ice Cream. All in all both the ice cream cone and paragraph can be delicious.

40

A Paragraph and an Ice Cream Cone
After Revising and Editing

The moist, creamy ice cream cone is a lot like a paragraph. The rich whipped cream topping is like the topic sentence because the topic sentence is rich with information about the paragraph. The cool texture of the ice cream is similar to the supportive details since the supportive details are in the middle of the paragraph just like the ice cream. The crunchy cone is a lot like the clincher sentence because the clincher sentence ends the paragraph just as the cone ends the ice cream. All in all, both the ice cream cone and the paragraph are alike because they both have three parts: the top, middle, and end.

Now that your students have had a series of in-depth mini-lessons on the writing process and paragraph structure, they should have a basic understanding of common writing terminology and editing concepts. In addition, they have been introduced to a framework for organizing their writing—the paragraph. With this foundation, students are ready to begin choosing their own topics and writing in response to literature.

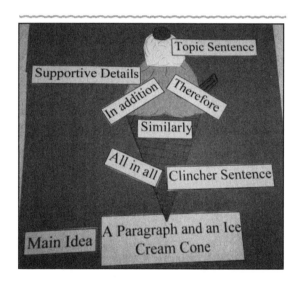

TEACHER TIP

If some of your students already understand paragraph structure, they can choose their own topic and begin writing. Students who have a strongly developed intrapersonal intelligence may prefer to work alone on the Lego model project. You can easily make adaptations for these students. On the next page is an example of a final product that was created independently.

The Lighthouse

A lighthouse and a paragraph have a lot of the same qualities. First, the very tip of the lighthouse has a knob on it. The knob has a light that draws attention to the ships in the area. This knob has the same job as a topic sentence. It draws attention to the lighthouse, and the topic sentence draws attention to the paragraph.

Second, the lights on the body of the lighthouse help guide the ships at night. These lights are similar to the supportive details in a paragraph. The supportive details help guide the paragraph so the reader understands what the paragraph is about. Third, there is a strong base at the bottom of the lighthouse to support the lighthouse just as a clincher sentence supports a paragraph by summarizing the main idea. In summary, a lighthouse and a paragraph have similar jobs and duties. They draw attention, provide support, and have strong foundations.

—Christina Burdge, Grade 6

Sandwich Cookie Paragraph

Crunchy, creamy sandwich cookies and paragraphs share common ingredients. Like the top part of the sandwich cookie, a paragraph's topic sentence provides a  delicious introduction to the main idea of the paragraph. Inside the paragraph, the rich, smooth filling, or the supportive details, support and develop the topic sentence. At the bottom of the cookie and at the end of the paragraph, the delectable experience ends with a final chocolaty crunch, or with a clincher sentence that restates the main idea in a powerful, new way. In summary, when biting into a scrumptious sandwich cookie, remember it has three parts just like a paragraph.

Paragraphs and Sandwich Cookies

Read the paragraph below. Highlight and label its various parts. Circle the transition words.

Crunchy, creamy sandwich cookies and paragraphs share common ingredients. Like the top part of the sandwich cookie, a paragraph's topic sentence provides a delicious introduction to the main idea of the paragraph. Inside the paragraph, the rich, smooth filling, or the supportive details, support and develop the topic sentence. At the bottom of the cookie and at the end of the paragraph, the delectable experience ends with a final chocolaty crunch, or with a clincher sentence that restates the main idea in a powerful, new way. In summary, when biting into a scrumptious sandwich cookie, remember it has three parts— just like a paragraph.

With a partner, discuss what you know about the paragraph. List five or more facts about paragraphs on the lines below. Share your facts with another set of partners. Add any new facts you learn from them to your list.

_____
_____
_____
_____
_____
_____
_____
_____
_____
_____
_____

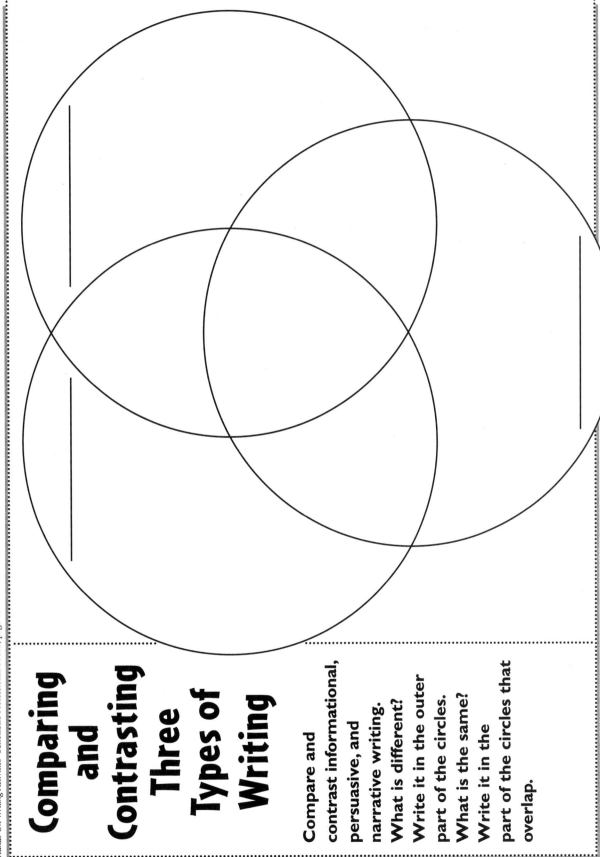

Comparing and Contrasting Three Types of Writing

Compare and contrast informational, persuasive, and narrative writing.

What is different?

Write it in the outer part of the circles.

What is the same?

Write it in the part of the circles that overlap.

Instruction Sheet for the Group Lego Project

Objective: To write a group paragraph explaining the relationship between your Lego model and a paragraph.

Social Skill: Working together.

Group Members' Roles	**Name of Group Member**
Person A: Topic Sentence/Task Master	_____
Person B: Supportive Detail #1/Gopher	_____
Person C: Supportive Detail #2/Encourager	_____
Person D: Supportive Detail #3/Recorder	_____
Whole Group: Clincher Sentence	

Directions: Complete each of the steps below. Put a check mark in front of each item after you have completed it.

_____ 1. Assign the group roles. Fill in the names of each group member who is responsible for the role assigned.

_____ 2. Complete the sheet titled "Prewriting Sheet for the Group Paragraph About the Lego Model." Take turns. Be sure each group member does his or her job.

_____ 3. Send the gopher to get the following materials:
4 large markers
1 off-white sentence strip
3 pink sentence strips
1 blue sentence strip
1 large paper clip
1 roll of masking tape

_____ 4. Using the marker, each group member will write his or her assigned sentence on the following sentence strips:
Letter A—Topic Sentence (off-white strip)
Write your name on the back.

Instruction Sheet for the Group Lego Project (cont.)

Letter B—Supportive Detail #1 (pink strip)
Write your name on the back.

Letter C—Supportive Detail #2 (pink strip)
Write your name on the back.

Letter D—Supportive Detail #3 (pink strip)
Write your name on the back.

Whole Group—Clincher Sentence (blue strip)
Write one name on the back.

Note: The first person finished in the group writes the clincher sentence.

_____ 5. Each group member hangs his or her sentence strip in the designated area.

_____ 6. The group goes on a gallery tour of the paragraphs.

_____ 7. The class discusses and evaluates the paragraphs.

_____ 8. Each group member takes down his or her sentence strip.

_____ 9. The gopher paper clips the sentence strips together and places them in the pocket folder.

_____ 10. The group completes "A Group Revision Activity."

_____ 11. The group uses ARMS to revise its paragraph.

_____ 12. Two group members write the final copy of the paragraph on notebook paper or the computer. Two group members draw a colored illustration of the Lego model and label its parts.

_____ 13. The group uses the rubric to evaluate its paragraph and the model.

_____ 14. Two groups exchange paragraphs and models and use the rubrics to evaluate each other's work.

Prewriting Sheet for the Group Paragraph About the Lego Model

Directions: Each member of your group has been assigned a particular role. Complete this sheet by taking turns and writing your assigned sentence.

Topic Sentence: States the main idea of the paragraph; shows what your model and the paragraph have in common.

Letter A—Write the topic sentence here: _____

_____

Supportive Detail #1: Shows one way in which your model is like a paragraph. (Remember to use a **transition** word if you need it. Circle the transition word.)

Letter B—Write supportive detail #1 here: _____

_____

Supportive Detail #2: Shows a second way that your model is similar to a paragraph. It must be different from supportive detail #1. (Remember to use a **transition** word if you need to, then circle it.)

Letter C—Write supportive detail #2 here: _____

_____

Supportive Detail #3: Shows a third thing that your model and a paragraph have in common. It must be different from supportive details #1 and #2. (Remember to use a **transition** word if you need it, then circle it.)

Letter D—Write supportive detail #3 here: _____

_____

Clincher Sentence: Summarizes the main idea of the paragraph in a powerful, new way. (Remember to use and circle a **transition** word that signals the end of the paragraph.)

Whole Group—Write the clincher sentence here: _____

_____

Rubric for "A Paragraph Is Like a _____"

Group Members' Names: _____

Peer Editors' Names: _____

Write the score for each item in the appropriate blank. Total the scores at the end.

1. The model effectively demonstrates its relationship to the paragraph.

4	3	2	1
The model effectively demonstrates its relationship.	The model demonstrates some similarities.	The model demonstrates few similarities.	The model demonstrates no similarities.

Score: _____ Group   _____ Peers

2. The model is labeled, neat, and detailed.

4	3	2	1
The model is labeled and is exceptionally neat and detailed.	The model is labeled and is neat and detailed.	The model is labeled but could be neater and more detailed.	The model looks as if it were thrown together at the last minute.

Score: _____ Group   _____ Peers

3. The paragraph has a topic sentence that states the main idea.

4	3	2	1
The topic sentence is interesting and clearly states the main idea.	The topic sentence states the main idea.	The topic sentence does not clearly state the main idea.	There is no topic sentence, or the topic sentence does not state the main idea.

Score: _____ Group   _____ Peers

4. The paragraph has at least three supportive details that make clear comparisons between the parts of the model and the parts of the paragraph.

4	3	2	1
The three supportive details make outstanding comparisons.	The three supportive details make clear comparisons.	The three supportive details make unclear comparisons.	There are fewer than three supportive details, and/or they are unclear.

Score: _____ Group   _____ Peers

Rubric for "A Paragraph Is Like a _____" (cont.)

5. The paragraph has a clincher sentence that is identified by a transition word and summarizes the main idea in a new way.

4	3	2	1
The clincher contains an appropriate transition word and powerfully summarizes the main idea.	The clincher contains a transition word and summarizes the main idea.	The clincher is too similar to the topic sentence and/or does not use an appropriate transition word.	There is no clincher, or it does not effectively summarize the main idea.

Score: _____ Group   _____ Peers

6. The paragraph has two circled transition words that clearly connect one supportive detail to another.

4	3	2	1
The paragraph has two circled transition words that clearly connect one sentence to another.	The paragraph has two circled transition words, but they do not clearly connect one sentence to another.	The paragraph has one circled transition word.	The paragraph does not have any transition words, or they are not circled.

Score: _____ Group   _____ Peers

7. The overall written comparison between the paragraph and the model is clear, logical, and easy to understand.

4	3	2	1
The comparison is exceptionally clear, logical, and easy to understand.	The comparison is clear, logical, and able to be understood.	The comparison is somewhat clear and logical, but is not easily understood.	The comparison is confusing and difficult.

Score: _____ Group   _____ Peers

Total Score: _____ Group   _____ Peers

| 28-26 = Excellent | 25-24 = Good | 23-22 = Fair | 21-20 = Needs improvement | Below 20 = Rewrite |

On the back of this sheet write one good thing about this paragraph and one thing the writers could improve.

Prewriting for the Paragraph Model Version 2

Directions: Each member of your group has been assigned a particular role. You must complete this sheet by taking turns and writing your assigned sentence.

Topic Sentence: States the main idea of the paragraph; shows what your model and the paragraph have in common.
Letter A. Create a topic sentence by filling in the blanks below.

A _____ has a lot in common with a paragraph.
　　　(what your model is)

Supportive Detail #1 Shows one way that your model is like a paragraph.
Letter B. Create supportive detail #1 by filling in the blanks below.

_____ the _____ is like
　　(transition word)　　　　　(part of the model that is like the topic sentence of a paragraph)

the topic sentence of a paragraph because _____

_____

_____

_____

_____

Supportive Detail #2 Shows a second way that your model is similar to a paragraph. It must be different from supportive detail #1.
Letter C. Create supportive detail #2 by filling in the blanks below.

_____ the _____
　　(transition word)　　　　　(part of the model that is like the supportive details)

represents the supportive details because _____

_____

_____

_____

_____

Prewriting for the Paragraph Model Version 2 (cont.)

Supportive Detail #3: Shows a third similarity between your model and a paragraph. It must be different from supportive details #1 and #2.

Letter D. Create supportive detail #3 by filling in the blanks below.

_____the _____
     (transition word)   (part of the model that is like the clincher sentence)

resembles the clincher sentence since _____

_____

_____

Clincher Sentence: Summarizes the main idea of the paragraph in a powerful new way. Remember your transition word that signals the end of the paragraph.

Whole Group. Create the clincher sentence by filling in the blanks below.

_____ _____
    (transition word)

_____

_____

_____

A Group Revision Activity

A Delicious Paragraph

[1] A greasy, good, delicious pizza has a lot in common with a paragraph. [2] For instance, the crunchy scrumptious crust is exactly like the topic sentence because it is at the top of the paragraph. [3] Lastly, the pepperonis resemble the clincher sentence. [4] The gooey sticky cheese represents the supportive details. [5] In conclusion, a pizza is like a paragraph because it has all the parts that are needed.

Group Questions to Help You Use ARMS

1. What word should be **removed** in the topic sentence? Draw a line through this word. What adjective can you **substitute** or use instead of this word? Put a ∧ below the word and write the new word above the word you crossed out.

2. What sentence needs to be **moved**? Write the sentence number here: _____. Circle the sentence and draw an arrow to where it should go.

3. Why doesn't the comparison in the second sentence make sense? What do you have to **add** to the sentence to have it make sense? Add words that will make this comparison sound right.

4. What needs to be **added** to the fourth sentence to show how the pizza's cheese and the supportive details are alike? Add the words that you need to make the comparison complete.

5. In sentence three, **add** information about how pepperonis resemble the clincher.

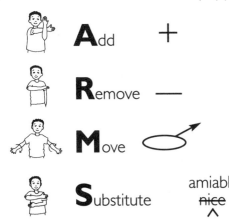

CHAPTER THREE

The Three Modes of Writing

In Pennsylvania, where I teach, schools are evaluated according to the Pennsylvania State Standards in writing by assessing students' writing in grades six and nine. The Commonwealth of Pennsylvania defines the three modes of writing as narrative/imaginative, informational, and persuasive (Pennsylvania Department of Education, 1998), basic categories that are probably similarly defined in your state. To provide practice in the three modes of writing and to introduce students to holistic assessment of their writing, I have them create food inventions. This is an activity that engages the students' imaginations and encourages them to look at everyday objects in a highly creative way. The students make and share their inventions, and then they use one of the three modes of writing to talk about them. This is a great activity to use in any writing class because it is highly motivating. Furthermore, it addresses the writing process, the three modes of writing, and the concept of assessment.

Mini-Lesson 7: Making Food Inventions

I love this mini-lesson! Your room will smell like peanut butter, and your colleagues might think you are insane, but your students will be extraordinarily creative and actively engaged in learning.

Objective: To create a food invention that will become a catalyst for persuasive, narrative, and informational writing.

Before preparing this lesson, it is very important for you to find out if any of your students is allergic to peanuts, as even the smell has the potential to trigger a serious—even fatal—allergic reaction. If you need to work around a peanut allergy, you will need to use your creativity to devise a different "recipe" for this lesson. Possible substitutes are cream cheese, whipped cream, strawberry jam, or apple butter.

Time: One or two 40-minute class periods.

Materials:
- 8–16 paper plates, one or two per group
- 8 plastic knives, one per group
- 1 large jar of peanut butter or substitute (put a large blob on the edge of each paper plate)
- Gum drops
- Miniature marshmallows
- Pretzel logs
- Graham crackers
- Licorice
- Flexible straws
- Toothpicks
- Eight large plastic bags

Preparation

Put several food items (except for the peanut butter), toothpicks, plastic knives, and flexible straws in the plastic bags before class begins. Provide at least four graham crackers and two pretzel logs per bag. Include a handful of the other food items. Since the peanut butter is the "glue" for the invention, put a large dab of it on the paper plate, which becomes the base for the invention itself. Have extra food items available in case a group needs them. Be sure to make your own invention to use as a catalyst for writing and as a model for the class.

Step-by-Step

1. Explain to your students that they are going to use food to create an invention, an original product that does not currently exist. Tell them that the inventions will help them learn about the three types of writing and to create stories, advertisements, or how-to paragraphs.

2. If you decide to create your own invention, you can make it in advance to show as an example of a finished product. In that case, you can describe what it is and how it works. Alternatively, you can work on your invention while your students create theirs, to model the process.

3. Have the students form groups of four and number themselves from 1 to 4. Assign the following group roles:

> #1 = **Gopher**—gathers and returns the materials
> #2 = **Reporter**—shares the invention with the class
> #3 = **Task Master**—keeps the group on task
> #4 = **Judge**—arbitrates the decision-making process about what
> kind of invention the group will create

4. Write on the board the steps the group needs to take in making the invention:

> **A.** Decide what you will invent (3–5 minutes).
> **B.** Begin building. Each group member will build one part of the invention.
> **C.** After the invention is complete, clean up the area. Leftover food items can be discarded—or eaten!
> **D.** Each group member should draw a sketch of the invention.
> **E.** Write the invention's name beneath the sketch.
> **F.** Have the gopher put the invention in the location designated by the teacher.

Mini-Lesson 8: Using Food Inventions as Springboards for Writing

Modeling is a powerful teaching technique. When I share models of various types of writing, the assignment moves from the abstract level to the concrete. Because students see examples and understand what is expected of them, they produce higher quality products.

Objectives: To share food inventions with the class.

To review narrative, informational, and persuasive writing as related to the food inventions.

To engage in the brainstorming and prewriting phases of the writing process.

Time: One or two 40-minute class periods.

Materials: ⚙ Student-generated charts with characteristics of the three types of writing
⚙ Overhead transparencies of a narrative, informational, and persuasive piece of writing about a food invention (pages 68–70)
⚙ Narrative/Imaginative Prewriting Sheets (pages 71–72)
⚙ Informational Writing Prewriting Sheets (pages 73–74)
⚙ Persuasive Prewriting Sheets (page 75)

Step-by-Step

1. Ask reporters to take turns describing their group's inventions to the class.

2. Remind students about the three modes of writing they have learned and discuss the charts describing the characteristics of each mode from the Great Paragraph Race. Tell the students that they will use one of these three modes to write about their food invention. Have students choose a partner to review and take turns naming and describing the three modes of writing. If students seem to have difficulty remembering the three modes, write the acronym NIP (narrative, informational, and persuasive) on the board as a prompt.

3. Next, show an overhead transparency of page 68, keeping the heading covered. Before reading the model aloud, tell students that you want them to identify what kind of writing the example demonstrates. Have them think about the purpose of this type of writing and make general observations about its characteristics.

4. Read the model aloud. Engage the whole class in a discussion of narrative writing. Afterward, hang up the student-generated list of the characteristics of narrative writing (see Chapter Two). Review these as they relate to the model.

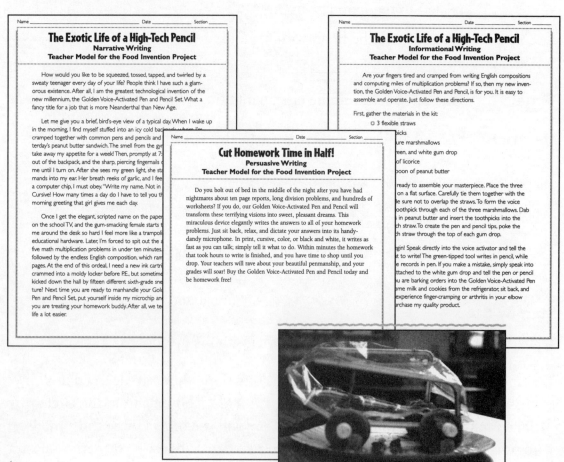

Name _____ **Date** _____ **Section** _____

Narrative/Imaginative Prewriting Sheet
A Story from Your Invention's Point of View

Purpose of Your Narrative: You are telling a story about a typical day in the life of your food invention from the invention's point of view.

Brainstorming: Before writing, visualize a day in your invention's life. Become your invention. Use your mind as a movie camera and picture everything that is happening around you. Then complete the prewriting sheet below.

Prewriting Activity

1. What are you? _____
(name the food invention)

2. Briefly describe yourself: _____
_____
_____

3. Write an attention-getting topic sentence that draws the reader into the brief story about an ordinary day in your life: _____
_____
_____

4. How do you feel about the way people treat you? List three (3) or four (4) of your strongest emotions.

   1. _____   3. _____
   2. _____   4. _____

5. List three (3) or four (4) interesting, humorous events tha[...] day in your life.

Event 1

Name _____ **Date** _____ **Section** _____

Informational Prewriting Sheet
How to Make the Food Invention

Purpose: You are writing to teach or instruct someone how to create and build your food invention. Step by step, show your do-it-yourself audience how to make the object.

Prewriting Activity

1. Name of the invention: _____

2. List the materials needed to make the invention:

   A. _____   E. _____
   B. _____   F. _____
   C. _____   G. _____
   D. _____   H. _____

3. Draw a sketch of the invention. Study the picture to remember the step-by-step process you used to build it.

[...]tion of the invention's purpose or usefulness:

[...]tting topic sentence that draws the reader into the paragraph:

Name _____ **Date** _____ **Section** _____

Persuasive Prewriting Sheet
Sell Your Invention!

- ☞ Create an eye-catching title.
- ☞ Appeal to the buyer's emotions.
- ☞ Begin with an attention-getting sentence that entices potential buyers to read the ad.
- ☞ Supply details that tell the buyers how your product answers their needs.
- ☞ Use powerful language and description to convince consumers to buy your product.

Prewriting Activity

1. Write an eye-catching title: _____
_____

2. Create an attention-getting opening sentence:
_____
_____
_____

3. Provide a brief description of what you are selling (your invention):
_____
_____

4. List at least three strong reasons why consumers should buy your product:
_____
_____
_____
_____

5. Write a sentence that will end your ad with a powerful punch:
_____
_____
_____

---

5. Repeat steps three and four with the informational and persuasive models.

6. Allow students to choose which of the three modes they would like to use in writing about their food inventions.

7. Encourage students to brainstorm as they engage in prewriting or drafting their pieces. If they need further guidance or prompting, distribute the prewriting sheets, reminding them to select the one that corresponds to the type of writing they have chosen to do.

Drafting, Peer Conferencing, Editing, and Assessing Food Invention Compositions

These are the steps I use to help students with drafting, peer conferencing, editing, and assessing their writing.

Objectives: To write the rough drafts of the food invention compositions.
To engage in a peer writing conference.
To assess a piece of writing.

Time: Three 40-minute class periods: one for drafting, one for peer conferencing and editing, and one for evaluating the final product.

Materials:
⚙ Praise, Question, and Polish Sheets (pages 76–80)
⚙ Rough drafts
⚙ Holistic Scoring Rubric (page 79), one per student
⚙ Pencils/pens

Drafting

Before students write the rough draft of the food invention compositions, distribute the sheet titled Holistic Scoring Rubric and have students place these in their notebooks. Reviewing the criteria for evaluation prior to drafting sets clear standards and expectations. The assessment sheet is based on the five characteristics of effective writing as defined by the Pennsylvania Department of Education: focus, content, organization, style, and

Name _____ Date _____ Section _____

Holistic Scoring Rubric

Circle One: Narrative   Informational   Persuasive
Rating System: 4 = Quality   3 = Satisfactory   2 = Adequate   1 = Needs Improvement

	4	**3**	**2**	**1**
Focus	• Demonstrates a clear purpose for writing that relates to the topic. • Presents ideas clearly.	• Demonstrates a consistent purpose for writing that develops the topic. • Most ideas are clear.	• Purpose for writing is blurry. • Some ideas are clear.	• Purpose for writing is not clear. • Few ideas are clear.
Content	• Contains specific information and details that relate to the topic. • Thoroughly develops ideas.	• Most information and details support the topic. • Sufficiently develops ideas.	• Some information and details support the topic. • Ideas need to be developed further.	• Very little information or details to support the topic. • Ideas are not adequately developed.
Organization	• Contains a distinct beginning, middle, and end. • Paragraphs develop one main idea. • Clear transitions between sentences and paragraphs.	• Has a recognizable beginning, middle, and end. • Paragraphs usually develop one main idea. • Most sentences and paragraphs have transitions.	• Weak beginning, middle, and/or end. • Few paragraphs develop one main idea. • Few transitions between sentences and paragraphs.	• No clear beginning, middle, or end. • Paragraphs do not develop one main idea. • Missing transitions.
Style	• Uses different sentence lengths and types. • Contains many, vivid, powerful words, not words such as "nice."	• Has some variety in sentence lengths and types. • Contains some, vivid, powerful words.	• Little sentence variety. • Few vivid, powerful words.	• Boring sentences that look and sound the same. • Filled with weak words.
Conventions	• Complete sentences. • Accurate spelling and punctuation. • Correct grammar and usage.	• Most sentences are complete. • Has few spelling and punctuation errors. • Most grammar and usage is correct.	• Some sentences are complete. • Spelling and punctuation errors are evident. • Problems with grammar and usage.	• Many run-ons, fragments, and sentence errors. • Lots of spelling and punctuation mistakes. • Incorrect grammar.

Writer's Rating: My overall rating for this piece of writing is (circle one)   4 3 2 1
Evaluator's Rating: My overall rating for this piece of writing is (circle one)   4 3 2 1
Teacher's Rating: My overall rating for this piece of writing is (circle one)   4 3 2 1
Reasons for Rating: _____

conventions (Pennsylvania Department of Education, 1998). These characteristics are the same as those outlined in the National Language Arts Standards. Provide one period of class time for students to draft the food invention compositions. Students who do not finish the drafts in class can complete them for homework.

Peer Conferencing and Editing

1. Divide the students into three groups based on the type of drafts they have written: narrative, informational, or persuasive. Students should select a partner within these groups with whom they will confer.

2. Then, have the partners exchange their papers and read them aloud to each other. The authors should comment on what they hear. Encourage students to identify what the writer does well and what needs to be improved. You can model a conference first.

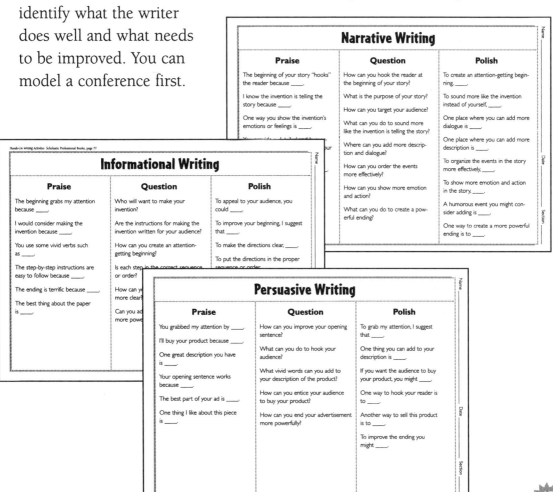

Narrative Writing

Praise	Question	Polish
The beginning of your story "hooks" the reader because ____.	How can you hook the reader at the beginning of your story?	To create an attention-getting beginning, ____.
I know the invention is telling the story because ____.	What is the purpose of your story? How can you target your audience?	To sound more like the invention instead of yourself, ____.
One way you show the invention's emotions or feelings is ____.	What can you do to sound more like the invention telling the story?	One place where you can add more dialogue is ____.
	Where can you add more description and dialogue?	One place where you can add more description is ____.
	How can you order the events more effectively?	To organize the events in the story more effectively, ____.
	How can you show more emotion and action?	To show more emotion and action in the story, ____.
	What can you do to create a powerful ending?	A humorous event you might consider adding is ____.
		One way to create a more powerful ending is to ____.

Informational Writing

Praise	Question	Polish
The beginning grabs my attention because ____.	Who will want to make your invention?	To appeal to your audience, you could ____.
I would consider making the invention because ____.	Are the instructions for making the invention written for your audience?	To improve your beginning, I suggest that ____.
You use some vivid verbs such as ____.	How can you create an attention-getting beginning?	To make the directions clear, ____.
The step-by-step instructions are easy to follow because ____.	Is each step in the correct sequence or order?	To put the directions in the proper sequence or order, ____.
The ending is terrific because ____.	How can you ____ more clearly?	
The best thing about the paper is ____.	Can you add ____ more powe____	

Persuasive Writing

Praise	Question	Polish
You grabbed my attention by ____.	How can you improve your opening sentence?	To grab my attention, I suggest that ____.
I'll buy your product because ____.	What can you do to hook your audience?	One thing you can add to your description is ____.
One great description you have is ____.	What vivid words can you add to your description of the product?	If you want the audience to buy your product, you might ____.
Your opening sentence works because ____.	How can you entice your audience to buy your product?	One way to hook your reader is to ____.
The best part of your ad is ____.	How can you end your advertisement more powerfully?	Another way to sell this product is to ____.
One thing I like about this piece is ____.		To improve the ending you might ____.

Hands-On Writing Activities Scholastic Professional Books, page 77

Hands-On Writing Activities Scholastic Professional Books, page 78

3. To help focus the peer conferences, distribute the appropriate Praise, Question, and Polish sheets to students. (I thank Cathy Cerveny, the 1997 Maryland Teacher of the Year, for introducing me to this strategy, which I have modified to fit the context of the food invention assignment.)

Explain that there are three columns on the sheet. The first column provides open-ended statements that a peer evaluator can use to "praise" or compliment the writer. The middle column contains questions the evaluator can ask to assist the writer with revision. The third column offers open-ended statements that help the evaluator make suggestions about how the writer can improve a specific aspect of the composition. Remind students that these sheets are to be used as a guide for the peer conferences. Not all questions or statements will apply to each composition.

4. Next, have students do the following, first to their own and then to their partner's paper:

A. Use ARMS to make further revisions (see Mini-Lesson 6 in Chapter 2).

B. Circle any misspelled words and label them **sp**.

C. Bracket and label run-ons, fragments, and sentences that do not make sense.

   [ ] R.O.   [ ] Frag.   [ ] S.S.

D. Use proofreading symbols to correct capitalization and end punctuation.

5. After students revise and edit the drafts, ask them to write the final copies of their compositions.

Assessment

To assess the food invention compositions, I designed a holistic scoring rubric, based on the criteria defined by the Pennsylvania Department of Education. It can be used to evaluate any of the three modes of writing. Instead of scoring the paper's focus, content, organization, style and conventions separately, compositions are rated on the "overall use of the five characteristics of effective writing" (Pennsylvania Department of Education, 1998). Consequently, as the writer and other evaluators use the Holistic Scoring Rubric, they must consider the quality of the writing as a whole.

The scores for the papers can range from 4 to 1, with 4 being the highest. Generally speaking, a piece of writing earns a 4 if it consistently demonstrates

the characteristics of effective writing. If the composition often employs the five characteristics of effective writing, it scores a 3. When the writing is inconsistent or unclear, the paper receives a 2. If the author does not effectively communicate his or her ideas, the appropriate score is a 1.

Provide direct instruction for using the Holistic Scoring Rubric. Review the criteria for evaluation and explain the concept of holistic scoring. Before having students begin their self and peer evaluations, model how to score by reviewing several papers on the overhead projector. After the students evaluate the papers, they need to justify the reasons for their scores, either verbally or in writing. On the rubric, I encourage students to highlight the writers' strengths in one color and the areas that need to be improved in another.

Reflections on the Food Invention Activity

Throughout the food invention project students are engaging in problem solving and critical thinking. In addition, they create both collaborative and individual products while learning about the three modes of writing. These products show-case their talents and creativity, as the student examples that follow illustrate. How can we be anything but optimistic about the future when we witness the creativity of inventions such as *The Gravitizer*, which simulates micro gravity, or the *Hairbrush That Colors*, a voice-activated hairbrush that washes, dries, and dyes your hair? Hands-on activities that stimulate thinking and facilitate learning bring out the best in our students and make teaching the embodiment of wonder and surprise.

TEACHER TIP

Have your students photograph or draw colored pictures of their food inventions and create a bulletin board to display the compositions and illustrations. Allow class time for students to read one another's writing. You can review the three types of writing by reading some of the compositions aloud and asking students to classify them as narrative, informational, or persuasive.

How to Make the Grade Averager—
Food Invention Informational Writing

If you ever wonder or worry about your grades at school, the Grade Averager is the perfect invention for you. My invention, the Grade Averager, records and tells you your grades for all of your classes throughout the school year. It keeps track of your grades and can tell you what your average is in any one or all of your subjects. You can use the Grade Averager to evaluate your success or need for improvement in school.

The materials needed to assemble the Grade Averager are as follows:

    5 sugar wafers
    2 toothpicks
    4 marshmallows
    2 tablespoons of
        peanut butter

Assembling the Grade Averager is easy. First, spread peanut butter on the tops of four sugar wafers. Second, stack the five wafers, putting the one without peanut butter on the top. Next, gently press the wafers together. Then push the toothpicks halfway into the stack of wafers. Finally, stick the two marshmallows into the top of the toothpicks. Your Grade Averager is complete!

It is not difficult to use the Grade Averager. Simply state the subject and the grade you wish to record while gently squeezing the top marshmallows. When you want to know an average of your grades, pinch the bottom marshmallows and state the subject. The Grade Averager will tell you the average. Don't be surprised by the grades on your report card. Use your handy Grade Averager to find out how you are doing.

—Michael Blackwell, Grade 6

Get to School in Style—
Food Invention Persuasive Writing

Do you hate that long, monotonous ride to school on the dreaded "cheese-wagon?" Are you tired of the obnoxious fumes coming from the back of the bus? If you are sick of the daily ride to and from school, our "Hover Bus" is for you. This sleek invention will make your really boring ride literally vanish into thin air. Super speed is what gets you to school. Just tell the computer where you want to go and in a few seconds you are there.

Our amazing piece of machinery has all the latest technology, including free drinks at each seat (if you have time to drink one). Best of all there is no need for the mean, old bus driver. This vehicle runs on autopilot. Just get in, sit down, and take off. There are no more screaming engines to listen to. Your brief ride is calm and peaceful. All too soon you will find yourself at your destination fresh and ready for a great day. Buy a Hover Bus today and be "cheese-wagon" free.

—Jason Shughart, Grade 6

Conclusion

Forging a strong foundation for writing begins by establishing a positive class-room climate, an environment that fosters trust and success. Students need to know that their thoughts and ideas are valued and that they have the ability to write. Within this nurturing environment, it is important for students to examine their individual writing processes through reflection and metacognition. During the writing process projects, students engage in reflective thinking, which encour-ages active processing and aids retention (Caine & Caine, 1990). To meet the needs of a diverse population, writing curricula and activities must consider the multiple intelligences, various learning styles, and individual students' cognitive profiles (Green, 1999). Therefore, the hands-on activities described here are mul-tifaceted; each one addresses the visual, auditory, and tactile-kinesthetic learner.

In addition, these activities align with both national and state standards, as students definitely "use the writing process elements to communicate with different audiences for a variety of purposes" (IRA & NCTE, 1996).

Because, as we have observed earlier, the act of composing occurs at the synthesis level, it is essential to move students slowly up Bloom's taxonomy to ensure that the writing task's level of difficulty encourages learning (Wolfe, 1998). It is essential, therefore, to design activities such as building Lego paragraph models and drafting and revising group paragraphs before asking students to participate in more complex, abstract tasks. Hands-on projects such as food inventions facilitate learning in the most effective way—by doing rather than merely absorbing.

Although the mini-lessons here are simply springboards into writing, young people will enjoy and learn from them. When your students collaborate and engage in motivating activities that are supported by educational research, they have a greater opportunity to be successful in your classroom. They come to class excited to learn and ready to participate. The air is charged with energy, vitality, creativity, and laughter. All of us want to be in this type of environment. All of us want to experience the thrill, exhilaration, and joy of learning, teaching, and working together.

The Exotic Life of a High-Tech Pencil
Narrative Writing
Teacher Model for the Food Invention Project

How would you like to be squeezed, tossed, tapped, and twirled by a sweaty teenager every day of your life? People think I have such a glamorous existence. After all, I am the greatest technological invention of the new millennium, the Golden Voice-Activated Pen and Pencil Set. What a fancy title for a job that is more Neanderthal than New Age.

Let me give you a brief, bird's-eye view of a typical day. When I wake up in the morning, I find myself stuffed into an icy cold backpack, where I'm cramped together with common pens and pencils and the crust from yesterday's peanut butter sandwich. The smell from the gym socks is enough to take away my appetite for a week! Then, promptly at 7:48 A.M., I'm yanked out of the backpack, and the sharp, piercing fingernails of my owner dig into me until I turn on. After she sees my green light, she starts shouting commands into my ear. Her breath reeks of garlic, and I feel faint; but, since I'm a computer chip, I must obey. "Write my name. Not in print, stupid. Cursive! Cursive! How many times a day do I have to tell you that?" What a sweet morning greeting that girl gives me each day.

Once I get the elegant, scripted name on the paper, Math Net comes on the school TV, and the gum-smacking female starts tapping and bouncing me around the desk so hard I feel more like a trampoline than pricey educational hardware. Later, I'm forced to spit out the answers to twenty-five math multiplication problems in under ten minutes. This torture is followed by the endless English composition, which rambles on for five pages. At the end of this ordeal, I need a new ink cartridge. Usually I'm crammed into a moldy locker before P.E., but sometimes I'm dropped and kicked down the hall by fifteen different sixth-grade sneakers. Get the picture? Next time you are ready to manhandle your Golden Voice-Activated Pen and Pencil Set, put yourself inside my microchip and think about how you are treating your homework buddy. After all, we techies do make your life a lot easier.

The Exotic Life of a High-Tech Pencil
Informational Writing
Teacher Model for the Food Invention Project

Are your fingers tired and cramped from writing English compositions and computing miles of multiplication problems? If so, then my new invention, the Golden Voice-Activated Pen and Pencil, is for you. It is easy to assemble and operate. Just follow these directions.

First, gather the materials in the kit:

- 3 flexible straws
- 3 toothpicks
- 3 miniature marshmallows
- 1 red, green, and white gum drop
- 1 piece of licorice
- 1 tablespoon of peanut butter

Now you are ready to assemble your masterpiece. Place the three straws lengthwise on a flat surface. Carefully tie them together with the piece of licorice. Be sure not to overlap the straws. To form the voice activator, place a toothpick through each of the three marshmallows. Dab the marshmallows in peanut butter and insert the toothpicks into the straight end of each straw. To create the pen and pencil tips, poke the flexible end of each straw through the top of each gum drop.

Let the fun begin! Speak directly into the voice activator and tell the pen or pencil what to write! The green-tipped tool writes in pencil, while the red-tipped one records in pen. If you make a mistake, simply speak into the microphone attached to the white gum drop and tell the pen or pencil to erase. While you are barking orders into the Golden Voice-Activated Pen and Pencil, grab some milk and cookies from the refrigerator, sit back, and relax. You'll never experience finger-cramping or arthritis in your elbow again once you purchase my quality product.

Cut Homework Time in Half!
Persuasive Writing
Teacher Model for the Food Invention Project

Do you bolt out of bed in the middle of the night after you have had nightmares about ten-page reports, long division problems, and hundreds of worksheets? If you do, our Golden Voice-Activated Pen and Pencil will transform these terrifying visions into sweet, pleasant dreams. This miraculous device elegantly writes the answers to all of your homework problems. Just sit back, relax, and dictate your answers into its handy-dandy microphone. In print, cursive, color, or black and white, it writes as fast as you can talk; simply tell it what to do. Within minutes the homework that took hours to write is finished, and you have time to shop until you drop. Your teachers will rave about your beautiful penmanship, and your grades will soar! Buy the Golden Voice-Activated Pen and Pencil today and be homework free!

Narrative/Imaginative Prewriting Sheet
A Story from Your Invention's Point of View

Purpose of Your Narrative: You are telling a story about a typical day in the life of your food invention from the invention's point of view.

Brainstorming: Before writing, visualize a day in your invention's life. Become your invention. Use your mind as a movie camera and picture everything that is happening around you. Then complete the prewriting sheet below.

Prewriting Activity

1. What are you? _____
(name the food invention)

2. Briefly describe yourself: _____
_____
_____

3. Write an attention-getting topic sentence that draws the reader into the brief story about an ordinary day in your life: _____
_____
_____

4. How do you feel about the way people treat you? List three (3) or four (4) of your strongest emotions.

    1. _____   3. _____

    2. _____   4. _____

5. List three (3) or four (4) interesting, humorous events that occur during a typical day in your life.

Event 1

Narrative/Imaginative Prewriting Sheet
A Story from Your Invention's Point of View (cont.)

Event 2

Event 3

Event 4

6. What do people say to you? _____

_____

_____

_____

7. What are some things you would like to say to your owners? _____

_____

_____

_____

8. How will your story end? _____

_____

_____

Informational Prewriting Sheet
How to Make the Food Invention

Purpose: You are writing to teach or instruct someone how to create and build your food invention. Step by step, show your do-it-yourself audience how to make the object.

Prewriting Activity

1. Name of the invention: _____

2. List the materials needed to make the invention:

   A. _____   E. _____

   B. _____   F. _____

   C. _____   G. _____

   D. _____   H. _____

3. Draw a sketch of the invention. Study the picture to remember the step-by-step process you used to build it.

4. Give a brief explanation of the invention's purpose or usefulness:

   _____

   _____

5. Write an attention-getting topic sentence that draws the reader into the paragraph:

   _____

   _____

Informational Prewriting Sheet
How to Make the Food Invention (cont.)

6. List the steps to create the invention (What did you do first? Second? Third?) or draw pictures of each step on a separate sheet of paper.

Step 1

Step 2

Step 3

Step 4

Step 5

Step 6

7. Write a clincher sentence that ends the paragraph with a powerful punch (perhaps give a great reason to use the product or invention).

_____

_____

_____

Persuasive Prewriting Sheet
Sell Your Invention!

⬡ Create an eye-catching title.

⬡ Appeal to the buyer's emotions.

⬡ Begin with an attention-getting sentence that entices potential buyers to read the ad.

⬡ Supply details that tell the buyers how your product answers their needs.

⬡ Use powerful language and description to convince consumers to buy your product.

Prewriting Activity

1. Write an eye-catching title: _____

_____

2. Create an attention-getting opening sentence:

_____

_____

_____

3. Provide a brief description of what you are selling (your invention):

_____

_____

4. List at least three strong reasons why consumers should buy your product:

_____

_____

_____

_____

5. Write a sentence that will end your ad with a powerful punch:

_____

_____

_____

Name _____ Date _____ Section _____

Narrative Writing

Praise

The beginning of your story "hooks" the reader because _____.

I know the invention is telling the story because _____.

One way you show the invention's emotions or feelings is _____.

You provide a detailed and humorous description of the events in your daily life by _____.

My favorite line of dialogue is _____.

I like the way the story ends because _____.

Question

How can you hook the reader at the beginning of your story?

What is the purpose of your story?

How can you target your audience?

What can you do to sound more like the invention is telling the story?

Where can you add more description and dialogue?

How can you order the events more effectively?

How can you show more emotion and action?

What can you do to create a powerful ending?

Polish

To create an attention-getting beginning, _____.

To sound more like the invention instead of yourself, _____.

One place where you can add more dialogue is _____.

One place where you can add more description is _____.

To organize the events in the story more effectively, _____.

To show more emotion and action in the story, _____.

A humorous event you might consider adding is _____.

One way to create a more powerful ending is to _____.

Informational Writing

Praise

The beginning grabs my attention because _____.

I would consider making the invention because _____.

You use some vivid verbs such as _____.

The step-by-step instructions are easy to follow because _____.

The ending is terrific because _____.

The best thing about the paper is _____.

Question

Who will want to make your invention?

Are the instructions for making the invention written for your audience?

How can you create an attention-getting beginning?

Is each step in the correct sequence or order?

How can you make the directions more clear?

Can you add some vivid verbs or more powerful adjectives?

Polish

To appeal to your audience, you could _____.

To improve your beginning, I suggest that _____.

To make the directions clear, _____.

To put the directions in the proper sequence or order, _____.

To improve your language and wording, _____.

To end the paper in a powerful way, _____.

Persuasive Writing

Praise

You grabbed my attention by _____.

I'll buy your product because _____.

One great description you have is _____.

Your opening sentence works because _____.

The best part of your ad is _____.

One thing I like about this piece is _____.

Question

How can you improve your opening sentence?

What can you do to hook your audience?

What vivid words can you add to your description of the product?

How can you entice your audience to buy your product?

How can you end your advertisement more powerfully?

Polish

To grab my attention, I suggest that _____.

One thing you can add to your description is _____.

If you want the audience to buy your product, you might _____.

One way to hook your reader is to _____.

Another way to sell this product is to _____.

To improve the ending you might _____.

Holistic Scoring Rubric

Circle One: **Narrative**　　**Informational**　　**Persuasive**

Rating System: 4 = Quality　　3 = Satisfactory　　2 = Adequate　　1 = Needs Improvement

	4	3	2	1
Focus	• Demonstrates a clear purpose for writing that relates to the topic. • Presents ideas clearly.	• Demonstrates a consistent purpose for writing that develops the topic. • Most ideas are clear.	• Purpose for writing is blurry. • Some ideas are clear.	• Purpose for writing is not clear. • Few ideas are clear.
Content	• Contains specific information and details that relate to the topic. • Thoroughly develops ideas.	• Most information and details support the topic. • Sufficiently develops ideas.	• Some information and details support the topic. • Ideas need to be developed further.	• Very little information or details to support the topic. • Ideas are not adequately developed.
Organization	• Contains a distinct beginning, middle, and end. • Paragraphs develop one main idea. • Clear transitions between sentences and paragraphs.	• Has a recognizable beginning, middle, and end. • Paragraphs usually develop one main idea. • Most sentences and paragraphs have transitions.	• Weak beginning, middle, and/or end. • Few paragraphs develop one main idea. • Few transitions between sentences and paragraphs.	• No clear beginning, middle, or end. • Paragraphs do not develop one main idea. • Missing transitions.
Style	• Uses different sentence lengths and types. • Contains many, vivid, powerful words, not words such as "nice."	• Has some variety in sentence lengths and types. • Contains some, vivid, powerful words.	• Little sentence variety. • Few vivid, powerful words.	• Boring sentences that look and sound the same. • Filled with weak words.
Conventions	• Complete sentences. • Accurate spelling and punctuation. • Correct grammar and usage.	• Most sentences are complete. • Has few spelling and punctuation errors. • Most grammar and usage is correct.	• Some sentences are complete. • Spelling and punctuation errors are evident. • Problems with grammar and usage.	• Many run-ons, fragments, and sentence errors. • Lots of spelling and punctuation mistakes. • Incorrect grammar.

Writer's Rating: My overall rating for this piece of writing is (circle one)　　4 3 2 1

Evaluator's Rating: My overall rating for this piece of writing is (circle one)　　4 3 2 1

Teacher's Rating: My overall rating for this piece of writing is (circle one)　　4 3 2 1

Reasons for Rating: _____

_____

Bibliography

Armstrong, T. (1994). *Multiple Intelligences in the Classroom*. Alexandria, VA: Association for Supervision and Curriculum Development.

Atwell, N. (1987). *In the Middle: Writing, Reading, and Learning With Adolescents*. Portsmouth, NH: Heinemann.

Bright, R. (1995). *Writing Instruction in the Intermediate Grades: What Is Said, What Is Done, What Is Understood*. Newark, DE: International Reading Association.

Caine, G. & Caine, R.N. (1990, October). Understanding a Brain-based Approach to Learning and Teaching. *Educational Leadership, 48*(2), 66-70.

Calkins, L.M. (1986). *The Art of Teaching Writing*. Portsmouth, NH: Heinemann.

Erickson, K. (2000, January 28). *What Does a 'Brain-Compatible' Classroom Look Like?: Eight Components and Instructional Strategies*. [Online] Available: http://www.davenport. k12.ia. us/~dcsd/curriculum/braincom.htm.

Fender, G. (1990). *Learning to Strengthen Skills and Brain Power*. Nashville, TN: Incentive Publications, Inc.

Green, F. (1999, Summer). Brain and Learning Research: Implications for Meeting the Needs of Diverse Learners. *Education,119*(4), 682-687.

International Reading Association and National Council of Teachers of English. (1996). *Standards for the English Language Arts*. Newark, DE and Urbana, IL: Authors.

Jensen, E. (1998). *Teaching With the Brain in Mind*. Alexandria, VA: Association for Supervision and Curriculum Development.

Johnson, D.W. & Johnson, R.T. (1994). *Learning Together and Alone*. Needham Heights, MA: Allyn and Bacon.

Kagan, S. (1994). *Cooperative Learning*. San Clemente, CA: Kagan Cooperative Learning.

Nicholson-Nelson, K. (1998). *Developing Students' Multiple Intelligences*. New York: Scholastic Professional Books.

Parnell, D. (1996, March). Cerebral Context. *Vocational Education Journal*, 71(3), 18-22.

Pennsylvania Department of Education. (1998). *PSSA Classroom Connections: Aligning Standards, Curriculum, Instruction, and Assessment*. Harrisburg, PA: Author.

Routman, R. (1991). *Invitations: Changing as Teachers and Learners K-12*. Portsmouth, NH: Heinemann.

Sousa. D.A. (1995). *How the Brain Learns*. Reston, VA: National Association of Secondary School Principals.

Southwest Educational Development Laboratory. (1997, Winter). How Can Research on the Brain Iinform Education? *Classroom Compass, 3*(2), 1-7.

Tomlinson, C.A. & Kalbfleisch, M.L. (1998, November). Teach me, Teach my Brain: A Call for Differentiated Classrooms. *Educational Leadership*, 56(3), 52-55.

Wolfe, P. (1998, November). Revisiting Effective Teaching. *Educational Leadership*, 56(3), 61-64.